Pagan Portals
Sun Magic

Pagan Portals
Sun Magic

Rachel Patterson

Winchester, UK
Washington, USA

First published by Moon Books, 2019
Moon Books is an imprint of John Hunt Publishing Ltd., No. 3 East Street, Alresford
Hampshire SO24 9EE, UK
office1@jhpbooks.net
www.johnhuntpublishing.com
www.moon-books.net

For distributor details and how to order please visit the 'Ordering' section on our website.

Text copyright: Rachel Patterson 2018

ISBN: 978 1 78904 101 9
978 1 78904 102 6 (ebook)
Library of Congress Control Number: 2018950264

A CIP catalogue record for this book is available from the British Library.

Design: Stuart Davies

UK: Printed and bound by CPI Group (UK) Ltd, Croydon, CR0 4YY
US: Printed and bound by Thomson Shore, 7300 West Joy Road, Dexter, MI 48130

We operate a distinctive and ethical publishing philosophy in
all areas of our business, from our global network of authors to
production and worldwide distribution.

Contents

Who Am I?

I am a witch ... have been for a very long time. I am also a working wife and mother who has been lucky enough to write and have published a book or thirteen. I love to learn, I love to study and have done so from books, online resources, schools and wonderful mentors over the years and continue to learn every day but have learnt the most from getting outside and doing it.

I like to laugh, bake and eat cake ...

I am High Priestess of the Kitchen Witch Coven and an Elder at the online Kitchen Witch School.

I also have regular blogs on:
Witches & Pagans – www.witchesandpagans.com/pagan-paths-blogs/hedge-witch.html
Patheos Pagan – www.patheos.com/blogs/beneaththemoon
Moon Books – www.moon-books.net/blogs/moonbooks/author/rachelp

My website and personal blog: www.rachelpatterson.co.uk
Facebook: www.facebook.com/rachelpattersonbooks
Email: kitchenwitchhearth@yahoo.com

Kitchen Witch School website and blog: www.kitchenwitchhearth.net
www.facebook.com/kitchenwitchuk

My craft is a combination of old religion Witchcraft, Kitchen Witchery, Hedge Witchery and folk magic. My heart is that of a Kitchen Witch.

Let the Sun Shine In …

I think sometimes as a witch the moon tends to get pride of place and the sun perhaps takes a back seat? But it is an incredibly powerful source of natural energy and magic. If you assign to the general school of thought about gender (more on that later) the sun is a very strong masculine energy that balances with the feminine energy of the moon.

How does the sun make you feel when it shines on a beautiful spring day after we have been subjected to rain, wind and snow? Turning your face and feeling the warm rays of sun. Having a picnic in the park or sitting on the beach on a warm summer's day. Makes you feel mighty fine, that's how it makes you feel! Now, I must admit I am not one to lie on a beach topping up my tan for hours, I am most definitely an English rose (and by that, I mean white and pasty). Besides, too much sunshine fades tattoos … However, I do appreciate the sunshine and I love being out in my garden when it is shining. And of course, I love working with sun magic.

The sun provides us with much nourishment not just in the form of Vitamin D which is necessary to keep us healthy but also in providing sunlight for plants and food to grow.

Magically, sunshine rays can be used to charge tools and crystals, to cleanse and purify pretty much any object or even yourself and focused through a magnifying glass onto paper or dry leaves it can even create fire. Just as we work with the phases of the moon for spell work, the sun has special times and phases that can be used to correspond with magical workings too. It also has a whole load of herbs, plants, foods and crystals associated with it.

And just as there is a tradition of drawing down the moon and her power into your body, you can do the same with the sun.

The Solar Cycle

Without getting too sciency (because I wouldn't understand it) let's have a look at the solar cycle. The sun is basically a big ball of hot gas that is electrically charged. The gas moves which creates a very powerful magnetic field. That magnetic field goes through a cycle. Approximately every eleven years that magnetic field flips completely causing the sun's north and south poles to swap over, then eleven or so years later it swaps back again. The solar cycle causes activity on the surface of the sun such as sunspots. The changing magnetic field activity affects the amount of movement on the surface of the sun.

At the beginning of a solar cycle there will be the least amount of sunspots and what is called a solar minimum meaning less activity. As time passes the activity increases. In the middle of the solar cycle when the sun has the highest number of sunspots the cycle is referred to as solar maximum (sounds like a Roman soldier). As the cycle progresses towards its end the activity decreases again, until a new cycle begins.

The sun also has indigestion, these solar flares are huge eruptions on the surface of the sun and these also increase with the solar cycle. A solar flare sends large bursts of hot gas, material and electrically charged energy out into space. These solar flares can cause lights to be seen in the sky from earth, shorten the lifespan of satellites, disrupt ship navigation systems and can even effect radio signals. Particularly large flares can also impact upon electricity grids. I did say the sun was powerful!

Solar cycles vary, some have more activity than others. Our clever science bods try and track, record and therefore predict how strong and how long each solar cycle will be. Being able to predict in detail can help them to do a 'sun weather forecast' which is technically referred to as 'space weather'. Being able to predict space weather can obviously help us to protect our radio communication and keep travelling astronauts safe (solar flares bring radiation with them, which is incredibly bad for people out for a spacewalk).

The sun also has wind (pardon you), and it is spectacularly impressive blowing in at around 600,000 to two million miles per hour. The solar wind flows along the magnetic lines of force; some charged particles fly down into Earth's atmosphere and create beautiful colours of red and green. These colours are the Northern and Southern lights (Aurora Borealis and Aurora Australis). You will usually have to be standing near to the North or South Pole to see them though.

Every 1.5 millionths of a second the sun releases more energy than every single human being put together consumes in an entire year. That is quite impressive.

The heat from the sun influences the environments of all the planets, moons, asteroids and comets in our solar system. This is one serious dude. It can create that amount of energy because it is basically an enormous ball of hydrogen held together by gravity causing a huge amount of pressure inside it. Hydrogen atoms collide with each other with enough force to create helium. Which means if the sun were to talk it would probably have a high squeaky voice … This process is called nuclear fusion, the atoms continually collide with each other creating a chain reaction that happens over and over and over … and you get the idea. The energy builds and can get as hot as 27 million degrees Fahrenheit in the core (ain't no sun factor for that). The energy travels outwards and on to the photosphere where it sends out heat, charged particles and light. This energy is what allows us to live on the Earth.

Thankfully the magnetic field around Mother Earth and her atmosphere protects us from most of the sun blasts. Otherwise it would get pretty hot and melty on our planet.

Everything in the solar system is continually on the move; the solar system includes the sun, nine planets and their moons, comets and asteroids. Collectively these are called celestial bodies. Sitting comfortably in the centre is the sun. It takes the sun twenty-five days to spin completely around. The earth, which is the third planet from the sun, takes twenty-four hours to rotate, i.e. a day and a night. As the earth rotates it revolves around the sun. It takes the Earth one full year (if you want to be picky 365¼ days) to completely orbit the sun. As the earth orbits the sun, the moon orbits the earth. Do you feel dizzy yet?

Sun Phases for Magic

And just like the moon, the sun has phases which can be used to tie in with your magical workings to add an extra boost of power. The sun measures time, where it sits in the sky denotes what time of the day it is, and a sun dial would be quite useless without the sun to cast a shadow! I also think the point between night and day and vice versa, that moment of hand over is quite special.

Sunrise – Basically when the sun wakes up and peers over the horizon. This phase is all about new beginnings, changes, health, employment, renewal, resurrection and finding the right direction. It can also be very cleansing.

The morning – This is when the sun is growing in strength, so it brings the magical power for growth, positive energy, resolutions, courage, harmony, happiness, strength, activity, building projects and plans, prosperity and expansion of ideas.

High noon – When the sun reaches its peak in the sky at midday – work magic for health, physical energy, wisdom and knowledge. It is also a good time to pop your tools or crystals out that need charging. (Note: some crystals can fade in strong sunlight so check first before putting them out.)

The afternoon – The sun is heading back down, and the energy now is good for working on business matters, communication, clarity, travel, exploring and anything professional.

Sunset – As the sun takes itself off down below the horizon, work magic for removing depression, stress and confusion, letting go, releasing or finding out the truth of a situation.

Magical Properties of the Sun

If you want to work with the overall magic of the sun these are some of the intents that it can help lend its energy to:

Success
Empowerment
Ambition
Enlightenment
Goals
Generosity
Spirituality
Male energy
Health
Vitality
The Gods
Joy
Freedom
Leadership
Matters of the heart
Creativity
Friendship
Growth
Personal fulfilment
Self-confidence
Wealth
Individuality
Pride
Energy
Power

Sunday

The second day of the weekend, and the last day of the week or in some beliefs ... the first day of the week. Sunday gets its name from ... the sun! The days of the week get their names from Hellenistic astrology. Seven planets being Saturn, Jupiter, Mars, the Sun, Venus, Mercury and the Moon each lent their name and energy to an hour of the day. The planet that was reigning during the first hour of any day of the week gave its name to that day. The Romans originally used an eight-day nundinal cycle but liked the idea and took on the seven-day week at some point during the first or second century, and as Romans like to do, they gave them the Roman names. The Germanic people also jumped on the idea taking it from the Romans but obviously changed the names of the days to suit them, changing them to Teutonic deities. The Latin Dies Solis became Sunday.

Before 1250ish (the year not the hour) the English word was sunedai which evolved into Sunnandaeg which literally means suns' day. Old Saxon used the term Sunnandæg and Old Norse was sunnudagr. All variations on a theme.

In most of the Indian languages the word for Sunday is either Ravivāra or Adityavāra, vāra means day and Aditya and Ravi are both a manner of addressing Surya the Sun and Suryadeva the main solar deity.

The modern Greek word Κυριακή, is derived from Greek: Κύριος which means 'Kyrios, Lord'; a day to mark the resurrection of Jesus, therefore 'the Lord's Day'.

Sunday was a day for the ancient Romans to worship the Sun god and they would pray at dawn to catch the first rays of sun for the day.

It was apparently a Roman Emperor (the first of Rome's Christian Emperors) that decided Sunday would be a day of rest.

Shabbat or Sabbath is the day of rest and seventh day of the week in Judaism. But the name has also been used by other traditions as a day of rest and of course modern pagans use the term sabbat for the eight festivals celebrating the equinoxes and solstices.

The usual calculation of a calendar day is measured from midnight to midnight but from the second century CE until 1925 the day was calculated from noon to noon. Ancient civilisations would often use dawn to dawn, counting the succession of days or suns. Later on, the Babylonians, Greeks and Jews used sunset to sunset. The Teutons counted the nights and it is from them that the term fortnight began, being fourteen days. Ancient Babylonians and other cultures liked to divide the day into watches. The length of each watch would vary depending on the time of year. In summer the watches were longer, in winter they were shorter, now we call them seasonal or temporal hours. They corresponded to the length of time the sun was above the horizon, maximum in summer and minimum in winter. The invention of mechanical clocks changed it all!

It was believed by most cultures that the seasons related to the sun and could be determined by observing the solar movements.

Sun Gender

Let's go with generally the sun is seen as masculine and the moon as female. I say generally because in some cultures and myths it is reversed and in some it has no gender at all. You really have to follow your own intuition on this one. I am going to cover myths and other beliefs in this book, but my personal view is that the sun is a masculine energy and the moon female, it works for me, it might not for you. I could be wrong, or right … let's be honest no one knows for sure and at the end of the day it is a big hot fiery star, it can be whatever it wants to be, I ain't gonna argue with it.

In a lot of myths, the sun and moon are seen as husband and wife or brother and sister. They are usually seen as opposites bringing balance. I don't think anyone is right or wrong and I don't believe our ancestors had a definitive answer either. Go with what works for you.

The sun is often seen as the active, energetic, warrior, go get 'em, action type of star. Full of oomph and abundance, creating warmth and helping the crops to grow. On the other hand, the moon can be seen as passive, ruling water and the emotions, no less powerful mind you.

If you check out the list of solar deities in this book (or anywhere else) you will find both gods and goddesses that are associated with the sun, so it seems no one could or would make a final decision.

I don't want to draw a definitive conclusion here and in fact I couldn't if I wanted to. It is your pathway and your belief; you are the only one that can decide what is right for you. Male, female, trans, Vulcan, alien, genderless or otherwise, the sun is a powerful source of energy and magic whether it has a gender label or not.

Sun Worship

Mankind has been worshipping the sun since he saw the first sunrise ... probably, because although I am not young, I really am not old enough to remember that particular event.

The sun was, and still is a source of light, power, energy and warmth. It was and is a source of life. You need the sunlight to grow the crops to feed the people. And when the sun was particularly hot, I suspect that many people wanted to know what they had done to make the sun so angry it would burn their skin ...

Across the globe cultures honoured sun deities and prayed that the sun would come up and present itself each day. From the Babylonians to the Native Americans and everywhere else in-between.

The sun has an ability to see everything, this would have given it great power (and still does) and may also be why we see so many connections throughout myths and legends between the sun and the image of an eye.

The gods of the skies and the heavens, those that ruled the sun, were worshipped and it seems often had chariots they rode across the sky. The Egyptian sun god Ra had a chariot that he drove across the heavens and the Greek god Helios was honoured by sending a horse-drawn chariot off the top of a cliff and into the sea (poor horses).

The ancient cultures of the Aztecs and Mayans worshipped celestial bodies and even created detailed calendars based on the movements. The Incans had a festival called Inti Raymi that has been suggested was celebrated to anchor the sun to stop it from moving further north, to keep the days longer and prevent them from shortening. Some cultures credited the sun as the creator of all things, giving birth to the stars. Early Persians from the cult of Mithra included sun worship and honouring in many of their rituals and ceremonies.

Archaeologists have uncovered a whole host of ancient structures, temples and buildings that seem to have been built to align with celestial bodies suggesting that the builders worshipped the sun, the moon and the stars.

During the early seventeenth century there was a bit of a scientific argument going on about the place of the sun in the universe. The Church at the time believed that the Earth was at the centre of the universe (because of man living on it) and therefore the universe must revolve around the earth.One of the key scientists of the day, Galileo, was condemned for his belief that this was incorrect ... science won out of course ... eventually.

There are many ancient sacred sites and structures that seem to have been built wholly or in part to worship the Sun or Sun gods, here are some of the most well known.

Stonehenge – one of the most well-known stone circles, Stonehenge in Wiltshire, England has, it seems, been a sacred site for an incredibly long time. No one really knows exactly what it was used for, but evidence does suggest that it has a link to prehistoric sun worship. When viewed from the 'heel stone' two large pits that have been uncovered align with the sunrise and sunset on the summer solstice. The suggestion is that a ritual procession may have taken place walking around the perimeter between the two pits. The sun at midday between the pits aligns directly with the centre of Stonehenge.

Temple of Karnak – A temple dedicated to the gods in Egypt is actually a city of temples dating from around 2055 BCE to 100 CE. This place is seriously huge. At the end of the yearly agricultural cycle the gods were thought to be exhausted and would require energy to rejuvenate them, understandably. The Opet festival was held at Karnak lasting for twenty-seven days. The central area was dedicated to Amun-Ra and the area around his sanctuary is called the Ipet-Sun which translates as 'the most select of places'. A further area is dedicated to his wife the goddess Mut and another to the god of war, Montu. There is also a temple to the child of Amun-Ra and Mut, Khonsu. In the east is an area set aside for Aten, the sun disk. During the reign of Hatshepsut (1479 to 1458 BCE) she renovated the main sanctuary and created a palace to the goddess Ma'at. The structure contains an open solar court above ground and subterranean rooms that symbolise the sun's passage through the Underworld.

Pyramids – It seems that a lot of the pyramids were built to align with the sun in some way. During the spring equinox at Giza in Egypt, the sun shines as it sets directly between the two largest pyramids and appears to sit on top of the sphinx like a crown.

Machu Picchu – an ancient Inca site found in Peru. The area appears to be a series of fortified sites and inns with signal towers along the highway. The suggestion is that the dwellings there were inhabited during the mid-fifteenth to early sixteenth century. It may well have been a palace for Pachacuti Inca Yupanqui. In the southern area is the 'sacred rock' also known as the Temple of the Sun. Near to the main plaza is the Intihuatana (Hitching post of the Sun), a ceremonial sundial that stands six feet (1.8m) high.

Teotihuacan – a Mayan city that can be found in Mexico. One of the first great cities of the western hemisphere, it is huge. Built many hundreds of years before the Aztec took it over, it is thought to have reached its peak between 100 BCE and 650 CE. There is a central road called the Street of the Dead and many buildings including the Temple of the Sun and the Temple of the Moon.

Newgrange – situated in County Meath in Ireland, Newgrange was built by Stone Age farmers some 5200 years ago, this passage tomb covered by a circular mound has an inner chamber reached by a passage that aligns with the rising sun on the winter solstice. It is also surrounded by ninety-seven kerbstones. It is thought to have been a temple for spiritual and religious worship.

Ajanta caves – in India there are thirty caves carved from the mountainside that form Buddhist temples dating back to the second century BCE. One of the caves aligns with the sunrise on the summer solstice, it contains a statue of Buddha and as the sun shines in, it illuminates Buddha on his seat.

Solstices & Equinoxes

Let's take a look at the solstices (not an easy word to say as a plural, way too many s's) and the equinoxes.

These are very important to the astronomical calendar as they mark the changing of the seasons and are a part of the earth's orbit around the sun.

We have two solstices a year, a summer and a winter one. The summer solstice occurs around the 21 June in the northern hemisphere and is the longest period of sunlight in a day, often called Midsummer or Litha in the pagan world. The winter solstice is around 21 December in the northern hemisphere and is the shortest period of sunlight in a day, known as Yule. The dates can vary by a day or two either way.

On the summer solstice the sun reaches its highest point of the year and at the winter solstice the sun at midday is at the lowest point of the year. The earth is actually tilted towards the sun during the summer solstice (in the northern hemisphere) which results in more sunshine and warmer weather. The sun is either farthest north or south from the earth's equator. The term solstice refers to either of the two points of greatest deviation from the sun's apparent annual path, from the celestial equator. Looking at the summer solstice, the North Pole is tilted about 23.4 degrees towards the sun, this causes the sun's rays to shift northwards by the same amount, the vertical midday rays are directly above the Tropic of Cancer. In the southern hemisphere the sun's vertical rays are at their southernmost position over the Tropic of Capricorn. Roll on to the winter solstice and the South Pole is inclined about 23.4 degrees towards the sun instead.

If you happened to be in the area north of the Arctic Circle on the summer solstice you would get sunlight for a full twenty-four hours, if you were south of the Antarctic Circle at that time you would be in complete darkness for a full day. Reversed, of course, at the winter solstice.

We also have two equinoxes each year. The spring equinox is around 20 March, or you might know it as Ostara and the autumn equinox is around 21 September (in the northern hemisphere) some modern pagans refer to this as Mabon. These mark the mid points between the summer and winter solstices, the point where the sun crosses the path of the equator and is positioned exactly above the equator smack bang in-between the northern and southern hemisphere. On each equinox, the day and night are exactly the same length. Hence the name, 'equi' meaning equal and 'nox' meaning night in Latin. The equinoxes mark the first day of spring with the coming days longer than the nights, and the first day of autumn with the nights becoming longer than the days.

Then we have an equilux (sounds like a Dr Seuss character). The equilux occurs a few days before the spring equinox and a few days after the autumn equinox. This is the time when the day and night are nearly equal, the sun appears as a disk in the sky and the top of it rises above the horizon before the middle. The sunlight is refracted by the earth's atmosphere. This gives the appearance of the sun rising before its centre is at the horizon, giving more daylight than you would expect.

For the southern hemisphere, the situations are reversed.

Solstice Magic

For the summer solstice you could work magic for:
Faerie
Communication
Intuition
Inspiration
Intellect
Movement of all sorts
Creativity
Transformation
Banishing
Manifesting
Reaching your goals

And at the winter solstice you might like to work magic for:
Honouring family and friends
Peace
Personal renewal
Meditation
Dream work
Balance
Knowledge
Loyalty
True feelings
Truth
Clarity
Transition
Planning
Long-term projects

Equinox Magic

The spring equinox brings good energy to work magic for:
New beginnings
Rebirth
Renewal
New life
Growth
Balance
Fertility (not just for babies! Fertility in new projects and ideas too)
Reconciliation
Resolving issues and conflicts
Protection
Self-control
Communication

And the autumn equinox is excellent for working with these:
Protection
Balance
Prosperity
Security
Self-confidence
Harmony
Balance
Fertility
Independence
Feminine issues
Love
Relationships
Sex magic
Health
Psychic abilities

Solar Eclipse

A solar eclipse is caused when a new moon moves between the sun and the earth, blocking out the sun's rays and casting a shadow over parts of the Earth. It is a rare event and each one can only usually be seen from a limited area. The shadow of the moon isn't actually big enough to cover the whole planet, so the shadow is always limited to a certain area. The area changes during the course of the eclipse as the Earth and the Moon are constantly moving.

Then you have a partial eclipse when the moon only partly covers the sun causing a half shadow (called a penumbra).

An annular solar eclipse is when the moon's disc is not big enough to cover the entire sun and the outer edges of the sun remain visible and form a ring of fire in the sky (sounds like a song title …).

A total solar eclipse happens when the moon completely covers the sun.

A real rarity is a hybrid solar eclipse or an annular total eclipse, this occurs when the same eclipse changes from an annular to a total solar eclipse or vice versa, along the eclipse's path.

You can only see a solar eclipse if you are on the planet Earth where the shadow of the moon falls, the closer you are to the centre of the path of the shadow the larger the eclipse looks. In most places a total, annular or hybrid eclipse will look like a partial eclipse because the darkest point of all solar eclipses is only visible from a small area.

A solar eclipse can only happen when the sun, the moon and the Earth are in a perfect or nearly perfect straight line. This alignment is called a syzygy. This alignment actually happens around the new moon every month. However, there isn't a solar eclipse every month because the new moon has to be in a lunar node. This means at two points where the moon's orbital path around the Earth meets the Earth's orbital plane around the sun, the ecliptic meet. It's all to do with the angle of the ecliptic. The sun needs to also be close to the lunar node, so it can form a near perfect or perfect line with the moon and the Earth.

I know this goes without saying but NEVER look at the sun eclipsed or not, without wearing proper protection over your eyes. The sun is a big fiery ball of hot stuff; it will burn your eyes and can cause huge amounts of damage. If you want to look at a solar eclipse use a pinhole projector (you will find instructions on how to create one on Google or YouTube).

Eclipse Magic

As an eclipse happens on a new moon it carries new moon magic, but as the sun and the moon are in the shenanigans together, it brings a combined and super-charged energy. It will amplify the characteristics of the sun sign that it happens in and also amp up all the magic of a new moon; new beginnings of all types, planning new ventures, taking the initiative, new jobs, change, positive energy, luck, growth and abundance. To me it also brings about changes, a huge big oomph of transformative power to bring change in quickly. As the sun emerges from the darkness it also symbolises rebirth and stepping from the dark into the light, so it is a good time to really take hold of those demons you have been stashing away (not literally, in your basement) and release negative patterns and move forward. As the moon blocks the sun, focus on any blockages you have and as the sun begins to emerge release them. Basically during an eclipse we experience a mini year, the sun is whole, then partially or completely dark then we see it again in all its glory, it has cycled through a complete year – the energy of a full circle. There is a weird stillness when an eclipse happens, as if everything in the world just comes to a grinding halt, just for a few moments. Relish that quiet time, it is very special, it is a 'between' time.

You don't have to be able to see the eclipse to work with the magic, it isn't visible in all parts of the world, but the energy is there to tap in to. Take into account the sun sign you are in when the eclipse happens as it will amplify that energy. If the eclipse is near or even on a solstice or equinox then it will carry the characteristics of that but ramped up, make use of it! Sit in meditation outside if possible and see what insights you can gain when the eclipse happens. Light a candle and send up a wish or your intent. Use the eclipse to set your intentions and lay out your goals. Set out some of your crystals or magical tools to charge them with eclipse energy.

It is a very special event and brings that little something extra with it so make sure you take advantage of this super beefed-up energy.

Solar Water

Eclipse water – Set out a jar or dish of water during an eclipse and let it soak up the energy. Then you can bottle it and use it at a later date. It can be used to water your plants that need a bit of a boost, to sprinkle on your spell work to boost the energy, drink a sip when you need an energy lift or before you work magic. Add it to your baking or cooking to send in the magic or pop a bit into your ritual bathwater.

Sunrise/midday/sunset – as above with the eclipse water, set it out during the phase of the sun you want to capture. Bottle it and use at a later date for the intent that corresponds to the phase you used to charge it under.

Solar water – for general purpose sun water, set out a dish or jar of water first thing in the morning and allow it to soak up the energy from the sun throughout the day. Take it in at sunset.

Obviously make sure your jar or dish of water is covered so that you don't end up with fly water ... yuck!

Journey of the Sun through the Wheel of the Year

I am not Wiccan, although I did my initial training in Wicca, so I don't necessarily work with this idea, but I am putting it in here as it may be useful to you ...

The Wheel of the Year is the journey through the calendar year marked by eight sabbats throughout. This journey is taken by the God and the Goddess within the cycle; it mirrors the stages of nature and the seasons. The goddess begins as a maiden and becomes a mother, she looks after her offspring and she grows in wisdom to become the crone, she remains a constant throughout the year, never dying or being reborn, only ageing. The God moves through the cycle but his is one of death and rebirth. He is at various stages a child, a lover, a guard and a protector. At the spring equinox/Imbolc the god is a growing youth, at Beltane he is a strong young man, at the summer solstice he becomes a father, at Lughnasadh/Lammas he is the sacrificial father and protector, at the autumn equinox he becomes the wise sage and at Samhain, he is back inside the womb. This of course reflects the sun and its transition through the year as the God.

There is also a tradition at both the summer and winter solstice, a battle between the Holly King and the Oak King. At the summer solstice the Oak King falls and the Holly King takes over to rule the dark half of the year. At the winter solstice the Oak King wins to rule the light half of the year. The Oak King heralds the returning of the lighter days, spring and all that it promises. The Holly King represents the darker days as we head into autumn and winter. It is a balance between light and dark and very much corresponds to the sun.

Sun Signs

We probably all know the answer straight away to the question 'what sign are you?'. But this usually refers to our sun sign i.e. our sign of the Zodiac. The date and time of your birth dictates your sun, star or zodiac sign, it is the position of the sun at that point when you entered the world. And the position of the moon at the time of your birth dictates your moon or lunar sign.

I am not going to delve deeply into zodiac signs and meanings here, but you can add oomph to your magical workings by tying the intent into the correct sun sign, i.e. when the sun is in a specific sign of the zodiac. The sun cycles through each sign of the zodiac throughout the year.

Aries: Mar 21–Apr 19
Taurus: Apr 20–May 20
Gemini: May 21–Jun 20
Cancer: June 21–July 22
Leo: July 23–Aug 22
Virgo: Aug 23–Sep 22
Libra: Sep 23–Oct 22
Scorpio: Oct 23–Nov 21
Sagittarius: Nov 22–Dec 21
Capricorn: Dec 22–Jan 19
Aquarius: Jan 20–Feb 18
Pisces: Feb 19–Mar 20

The list below gives some suggestions on what magic to work for when the sun is in a specific zodiac sign (the list is taken from my book *Kitchen Witchcraft: Spells & Charms*).

Aries
Work spells for: Courage, authority, leadership, power, the

forces, will power, new beginnings, challenges and protection.

Taurus
Work spells for: Stability, health, assistance, marriage, family, material gain, careers, financial stability and healing.

Gemini
Work spells for: Communication, neighbours, travel, siblings, transport, knowledge, education, activity, imagination, divination, wishing spells, luck and success.

Cancer
Work spells for: Family, home, domestic situations, gratitude, blessings spells, comfort, abundance, prosperity, love, luck and cleansing.

Leo
Work spells for: Courage, the arts, public speaking, fertility, childbirth, healing, influence, success, goals, removing obstacles, creativity and confidence.

Virgo
Work spells for: Employment, foundations, planning, organisation, financial planning, communication, clarity, precision, research, paperwork, details and healing.

Libra
Work spells for: Creativity, expression, partnerships, legal matters, balance, new love, new projects, truth and justice.

Scorpio
Work spells for: Luck, psychic abilities, mental issues, inner work, secrets, cleansing, reincarnation, past lives, karma, enemies, spirituality and magic of all kinds really.

Sagittarius

Work spells for: Travel, legal matters, publishing, healing, growth, spiritual relationships, creativity, co-operation, sharing, business success, transformation, inspiration, new beginnings, expanding, removing obstacles, releasing and meditation.

Capricorn

Work spells for: New business, new projects, planning, growth, organisation, foundations, ambitions, strength, health, banishing debt, clearing out, removing obstacles, rules, boundaries and elimination of pain.

Aquarius

Work spells for: Inspiration, innovation, clarity, social events, friendships, moving forward and solving issues.

Pisces

Work spells for: Dreams, astral travel, past lives, reincarnation, karma, psychic abilities, creativity, the arts and re-connecting with your spiritual path.

Sun Herbs and Plants

Within magic we often associated herbs, plants and flowers with planets or elements and I often wondered why or how it came about. It seems the English astrologer-physician Mr Culpepper may have been one of the key advocates. He associated plants with the planets that he thought best represented the healing properties they carried and the illnesses and diseases it cured. He also liked to link herbs to planets according to their colour or appearance, so golden yellow herbs that had a solar appearance would come under the sun ruling. For instance, any plants that had thorns or stings such as nettles and hawthorn would be placed in the Mars category, Mars symbolising the God of War.

The ancient Greeks also believed all remedies and healing plants had their own nature and characteristics along with astrological affinities. They would also associate the plant to a planet depending on the illness it treated and the corresponding energies of the planet.

The medieval Doctrine of Signatures also followed similar guidelines with plants and herbs, associating their looks and colours with the personality and energy of planets.

The sun covers all yellow and solar looking herbs and plants, herbal medicines that cover heart problems, bringing strength to the body, resistance poison, bringing warmth to the system, evergreens with a strong life force and all herbs and plants that are linked to eyesight; any plant life that restores energy, vitality and boosts the immune system. Stimulants and those that clear the lungs and respiratory tract, and all plants that relieve pain or inflammation were believed to be ruled by the sun as well.

Makes sense to me!

Here are some plants ruled by the sun, to get you started:

Angelica – Protection, healing, exorcism, divination, prosperity, luck, hex breaking, courage.

Also ruled by Venus and the element of fire so you get a double whammy of sunshine energy.

Ash – Protection, prosperity, dispels negativity, improves health, sea magic, dreams, love, intuition.

Also ruled by Neptune and both a fire and water element plant.

Bay – Protection, purification, strength, power, healing, creativity, spirituality, psychic powers.

With the element of fire, it is a hot one!

Benzoin – Prosperity, purification. Element – air.

Bergamot (orange) – Money, uplifting, success, Sun magic, banishing, purification. Also ruled by Mercury and the element of air.

Buttercup – Abundance, ancient wisdom, divination, protection, psychic abilities. Element – fire.

Calamus – Money, protection, healing, luck. Also ruled by the Moon and the element of water so a gentle Sun energy with this one.

Carnation – Healing, strength, protection, release, courage. Element – fire.

Cedar – Purification, money, protection, Goddess. Also ruled by Jupiter and the element of fire.

Celandine – Happiness, protection, release, escape, legal matters. Element – fire.

Chamomile – Sleep, dreams, love, calm, money, relaxation, purification, balancing. Element – water.

Chrysanthemum – Longevity, spirituality, protection. Element – fire.

Copal – Purification, love, protection. Also ruled by Jupiter and the element of fire.

Eucalyptus – Moon magic, sun magic, divination, dreams, healing, purification. Also ruled by the Moon and both the elements of water and air.

Frankincense – Purification, spirituality, relaxation, focus, love, abundance. Element – fire.

Hazel – Fertility, wishes, love, protection, luck, wisdom, divination, healing, inspiration, prosperity. Element – air.

Heliotrope – Dreams, spirituality, exorcism, protection, forgiveness, abundance. Element – fire.

Juniper – Love, exorcism, healing, protection, justice, stolen items, purification, psychic powers, clarity. Also ruled by Jupiter, the Moon and the element of fire.

Lovage – Protection, love. Also ruled by the Moon and the element of fire.

Mace – Purification, consecration, psychic powers. Also ruled by Mercury and the element of air.

Marigold – Psychic powers, dreams, protection, luck, happiness, gossip. Element – fire.

Mistletoe – Fertility, protection, love, health, dreams. Element – air.

Morning Glory – Divination, astral travel, psychic powers. Also ruled by Neptune and the element of air.

Myrrh – Protection, purification, healing, Crone, Underworld, courage. Also ruled by Mars and the element of water.

Oak – Healing, health, protection, money, fertility, luck, strength, vitality, power. Also ruled by Jupiter, Mars and the elements of fire and water.

Peony – Exorcism, protection, luck, happiness, blessings. Element – fire.

Rowan – Psychic powers, power, success, protection, love, spirituality, faeries, divination, healing, inspiration. Also ruled by Mercury and the element of fire.

Rue – Protection, health, healing, purification, balance, clarity, anxiety, hex breaking. Also ruled by Mars and the element of fire.

St John's Wort – Protection, health, strength, love, divination, happiness, abundance, truth. Element – fire.

Sunflower – Wishes, fertility, truth, integrity, luck, protection, loyalty, happiness. Element – fire.

Witch hazel – Protection, divining, balance, grief. Also ruled by Saturn and the element of fire.

Solar Tea Blends

If you have a garden full of flowers and herbs or a cupboard full of herbs and spices you can create your own herbal tea blends very easily.

Use one or two teaspoons of the herb/spice if using dried or a handful of fresh leaves, pour on hot water and brew for at least 5 minutes then strain. You can drink it warm or chill it and drink it with ice. It can also be used as a mouth wash, gargle or hair rinse. (Only keep for a maximum of 24 hours.) Herbal tea blends can also be used as floor washes.

Experiment with different herbs, flowers and spices and see which flavours you prefer. If you want it sweeter then drop in a teaspoon of honey or agave nectar.

If you are using plants picked from the wild or your garden, please make sure you have identified them correctly. If you have any medical problems or are taking any medication, please check that there are no clashes with the herbs. Herbs used in a medicinal or tea form can be extremely powerful and can have adverse effects with some over-the-counter medications. They can also react dangerously with some medical conditions. Be careful, be safe.

A few solar herbal tea blend ideas:

Chamomile and hibiscus
Elderflower and mint
Hibiscus and rose
Marigold and mint
Rosemary and hibiscus
Sage and lemon balm or lemon verbena
Strawberry and woodruff
Yarrow and mint
Lemon balm, ginger, sunflower and bay

Orange and mint
Strawberry and basil
Apple and mint

If you don't have herbs or flowers to hand then you can buy some really good herbal tea blends in the stores, conveniently packaged in tea bags.

Also try blending a black or green tea with herbs and flowers.

Sun Incense Blends

I think the best way to create any loose incense blend is by intuition. Get the intent you want in your mind and then browse your cupboards, see what jumps out at you. Let your intuition decide what goes into the mix. However, I have given some of my favourite solar blends below. Experiment and see what works best for you. I would also recommend using whatever you have to hand, grown in your garden or sourced cheaply from local stores. I don't see the point of ordering expensive ingredients from across the globe. My only diversion from this rule is to order resins such as copal and frankincense online because I can't grow it and I do think incense needs a resin as a base, it helps it burn longer. Do check if you order items online that they have been ethically and eco-friendly sourced.

Start with a base, a resin is good such as frankincense or copal. Adding a wood of some sort helps your incense to burn longer, if you are using home grown dried herbs the woody stems of herbs can be added in too. Then the choice is up to you, whether you go for the scent you like or for the intent. Incense can be made for prosperity, love, success etc. but you can also make incense to correspond with the sun or moon phase, a sabbat, a particular ritual or to honour a specific deity.

I also like to add a few drops of essential oil to my incense mix once I have finished it too, just to give it an extra boost of scent and power.

Remember as well that incense put together for magical purpose may not always smell particularly pleasant, it is the energies of the herbs that are important!

I would also suggest keeping it simple, too many ingredients and it gets complicated. Less is more as they say. And if you do use a resin, it will make a lot of smoke, remember to burn it in a well-ventilated area.

If you want to add solar energy to your blends, try creating them outside in the sunshine or by a window where the sunlight can add to the energy. Or create them on a Sunday.

With all the recipes below, I usually go with an equal amount of each ingredient but mix it up with dried herbs and plants or essential oils depending on what I have in store. For things like orange and lemon, I use dried peel but boost it with a couple of drops of essential oil.

Solar plexus incense blend
Fennel
Geranium
Jasmine
Lavender
Sandalwood

Sun incense
Frankincense
Cinnamon
Orange

Sun incense
Frankincense
Sunflower
St John's Wort
Orange
Marigold
Bergamot

Sun incense
Clove
Copal
Orange
Saffron

Sun incense
Cedar
Copal
Rosemary
Cinnamon

Sun incense
Frankincense
Cinnamon
Cardamom
Nutmeg

Sun incense
Frankincense
Sandalwood
Bay
Orange

Sun incense
Frankincense
Ginger
Bay
Red wine
Honey

Solstice incense
Orange
Grapefruit
Lemon

Sun Oil Blends

You can make up your own essential oil blends quite easily, although it may take a bit of experimentation to get blends that smell just as you want them to.

Start with a base oil such as olive oil, almond oil or I like to use coconut oil, for solar oil blends then sunflower oil would work well. It is safer to dilute essential oils with a base oil if you are going to use them topically especially if they are for use on children or the elderly. A 2% dilution is a safe guide, 1% for children. (Please consult a qualified aromatherapist if you are looking at using oils on children.) I would not advise using essential oils if you are pregnant, some are safe but personally I don't think it's worth taking the risk.

If I am creating a new blend, I like to put a drop of each essential oil in a little bowl first to see if the scents work together before I make up a bottle.

30ml (1 fluid oz) of base oil works well with about 12 drops of essential oil.

You can also make your own scented oils from fresh herbs and petals and because you use the power of the sun it adds solar energy to it. Take a base oil and add flower petals, herbs (just the leaves), spices (crushed) or citrus peel to the base oil, cover and leave to stand for a minimum of 48 hours on a sunny windowsill, giving the jar a shake every 12 hours. Leaving it for two weeks is preferable, four weeks is suggested but sometimes we are in a hurry! After you have allowed it to 'do its thing' on the windowsill, strain the liquid and throw away the herbs (put them on the compost heap or return them to the soil). If the oil does not have a strong enough scent, repeat the process with fresh herbs/flowers/spices until you get the strength of scent that you want.

Some ideas for solar herbal oil blends – add a few drops of

each oil to your base oil:

Solstice oil blend
Chamomile
Gardenia
Rose
Lavender
Yarrow

Solstice oil blend
Thyme
Rosemary
Vervain
Frankincense

Solstice oil blend
Lavender
Rosemary
Pine

Summer oil blend
Lemon balm
Orange
Sandalwood
Ylang ylang

Sunshine oil blend
Orange
Lime
Basil

Foods Ruled by the Sun

As with magical herbs being ruled by planets, foods also have associations with celestial bodies. Here are some that are ruled by the sun. Use them in magical workings; nuts and seeds lend themselves very well to this – add to spell pouches or witch bottles for instance. Or meals can be prepared in honour of sun energy or solar gods and eaten.

Cashew – Prosperity, energy. Element fire and earth.

Cinnamon – Success, healing, power, psychic powers, protection, love, focus, lust, spirituality, changes. Element – fire.

Corn – Abundance, luck, prosperity, offerings, fertility. Element fire and earth.

Dates – Spirituality, death & rebirth, offerings. Element – air.

Grapefruit – Happiness, spirit work, purification, depression, energy. Also ruled by Jupiter and the elements of fire and water.

Hazelnut – Protection, psychic powers, wisdom, fertility, Faerie, Healing. Also ruled by Mercury and the element of air.

Kumquat – Sun energy, luck, money. Element – air.

Lime – Purification, love, healing, protection, energy. Element – fire.

Olives – Spirituality, integrity, passion, fertility, healing, peace, protection, luck. Element fire and air.

Orange – Love, happiness, uplifting, generosity, purification, clarity, energy, fidelity. Element – fire.

Pineapple -- Chastity, protection, luck, prosperity, healing. Element – fire.

Rice – Prosperity, fertility, protection, rain, grounding, stability. Element air and earth.

Rosemary – Protection, love, lust, mental powers, exorcism, purification, healing, sleep. Element – fire.

Saffron – Happiness, energy, psychic powers, healing, fertility. Element – fire.

Sesame – Prosperity, protection, energy, strength, secrets. Element fire and earth.

Tea – Meditation, courage, strength, prosperity. Element – fire.

Walnut – Wishes, mental powers, clarity, fertility. Element – fire.

Wine (red) – Spirituality, offerings, happiness, love. Element fire and earth.

Crystals

Every full moon social media is full of memes advising everyone to pop their crystals out to cleanse, purify and soak up the moonlight … but I don't… and it isn't just because I don't like being told what to do …

I do put some crystals out on the full moon but not all of them. There are some crystals that I think suit the moonlight but others that I find work better by being put out in either the sunshine or even the rain and wind.

Which stones?

For instance, I put stones like moonstone (obviously!), quartz and blue lace agate out in the moonlight.

But for stones such as sunstone, topaz, tiger's eye, carnelian, amber and all the fiery stones, I like to put them in the sunshine so that they soak up the fiery energy instead.

And then we have watery stones, if it is raining then there are some stones that love being out in it such as amethyst, blue lace agate and lapis. (Note: don't put porous stones out in the rain … they may not be there when you get back …)

You can even take it further and separate them into the four elements and put out air stones on a windy day and bury earth stones (carefully and mark where you put them) in the soil. Fire stones would go out in the sun and water stones in the rain.

Air stones would be things like amethyst, citrine and turquoise. For earth, these stones might be agate, jasper and jet.

Obviously, some of the stones will fit into a couple of the categories and I also go by colour: yellow, red and orange stones go in the sun and white, blue and pale stones go under the moon.

Trust your intuition … but I prefer not to lump all the stones under the moon because it is incredibly powerful, and I personally feel that some of my crystals work better with sun, wind or water energy instead.

Go with what feels right for you ...

Crystals Associated with the Sun

Sunstone – This stone does what it says on the tin: Energy, potential, leadership, power, freedom, consciousness, openness, benevolence, warmth, strength, clarity, blessings, joy, happiness, nurture, good nature, abundance, independence, inspiration, fame, balance, prosperity, luck, enthusiasm, vitality, opportunities, de-stress and dispels negative energy and fear.

Citrine – Positive energy, joy, success, wealth, abundance, manifestation, will, perseverance, creativity, imagination, clarity, meditation, strength, goals, inspiration and warmth.

Clear Quartz – Amplifying, manifesting, healing, activation, enlightenment, consciousness, communication, clarity, clearing blockages, energy flow, positive energy and pretty much anything else, clear quartz is a good all-round crystal that can be programmed with any intent.

Goldstone – Ambition, drive, confidence, dreams, goals, joy, inner light, protection, warrior energy, grounding, healing, balance, harmony, creativity, sensuality, inspiration, reflects negative energy, consciousness and connection with the divine.

Golden topaz – Influence, generosity, strength, luxury, true love, fidelity, friendship, courage, wisdom, success, healing, soothing, stimulation, recharging, energy, joy, abundance, will, manifestation, creativity, intention, connection to the divine, faith, optimism, confidence, overcoming limitations and attraction.

Heliodor – Warmth, power, consciousness, well-being, knowledge, learning, leadership, decisions, assertiveness, confidence, strength, benevolence, power, hope, calms the nerves, relief, stability, optimism, honesty, balance, determination, drive, enthusiasm, finances, happiness, memory and protection against negative energy.

Sulfur – Vitality, energy, protection, purification, detoxing, un-hexing, dispels negative energy, healing and solar plexus work.

Zircon – Spirituality, balance, healing, self-love, love, clarity, grounding, energy, organisation, sexuality, dispel depression, protection, success and to increase alertness.

Gold (yep I know technically it is a metal and not a crystal) – Definitely a stone of the sun. Power, enhancing magic, boosting power, directing energy, illumination, success, knowledge, learning, responsibility, self-confidence, calming, dispel negative energy, transformation and amplifying.

Ruby – Encouragement, energy, passion, clearing the darkness, creativity, awareness, manifestation, stability, wealth, concentration, clarity, wisdom, focus, motivation, productivity, protection against negative energy and psychic attack, courage, joy, leadership, spirituality and power.

Rutilated quartz – Clarity, duality, perspective, antidepressant, healing, emotions, spirituality, cleansing, recharging, purification, energy, meditation, dispels negative energy, clarity, intention, direction and angel work.

Garnet – Energy, grounding, connection, clearing blockages, joy, vitality, love, relationships, strength, direction, progress, consciousness, actions, attraction, protection, healing and positive energy.

Pyrite – Wealth, luck, strength, motivation, connection, wisdom, action, aspirations, meditation, guidance, protection, self-confidence, prosperity, healing, intention, focus, gratitude and abundance.

Tiger's Eye – This stone combines both sun and earth energy and was used to transmit power to the sun god Ra. Success, energy, power, spirituality, attraction, luck, money, wealth, truth, courage, strength, passion, vitality, clarity, joy, grounding, understanding, balance, insight, will, centring, information, divination and protection.

Topaz – Also said to be filled with the energy of the sun god Ra. Clarity, protection, strength, power, invisibility, spirituality, intelligence, creativity, wisdom, wealth, love, success, understanding, compassion, kindness, empathy, communication, abundance, planning, anti-depression, emotions and to help sleep.

Amber – Manifestation, energy, conductivity, luck, life, beauty, power, desires, clarity, wisdom, balance, purification, protection, psychic shielding, healing, calm, patience, love, sensuality, abundance, vitality, joy, soothing, strength and calming.

Diamond – Cleansing, removing obstacles, self-respect, love, emotions, relationships, abundance, balance, clarity, anti-jealousy, amplifying, courage, hope, confidence, meditation, consciousness, strength, protection, luck and spirituality.

Sun Crystal Grid

A crystal grid is a geometric pattern of crystals, each one charged with intent and adding its own power to the other crystals in the grid. I think crystal grids are one of the most powerful crystal set-ups you can use, they utilise sacred geometry and all sorts of sciency stuff including tapping into the universal energy and ley lines, but we will stick with how to make them and leave the 'why they work' and just call it magic ...

First of all, you need to decide what your intent is for creating the grid. Grids can be created for just about any purpose. Make sure your intent is clear and specific though because you don't want the power wandering off in unspecified directions!

You can draw out a sacred geometry pattern to work from or print one from the net, but I prefer to work intuitively, whatever way works best for you. A hexagon is a good shape to start with, but you can also use triangles, squares, circles, stars, a spiral or the infinity symbol. As we are focusing on solar energy here, then, a sun shape layout would work perfectly, a circle with rays of crystals around it perhaps? And of course, if you can set it up outside in the sunshine to be charged by solar rays that would make it even more powerful.

I start with the centre stone, this creates the key point or the power stone, this stone is the amplifier, the connector for the whole grid. I like to use a larger crystal as the centre stone, whilst this isn't absolutely essential it does seem to conduct the power more efficiently.

Don't feel you can't create a crystal grid if you can't afford to buy a big crystal, even if you only have a small selection of tumble stones you can still create an effective grid.

How many surrounding stones you use is up to you and the size of grid you want to create. I also like to charge each stone with the intent as I place it. Start with a basic design and see where your intuition takes you – there is no right or wrong.

To choose the crystals for your grid you can go with your instinct or look up the meanings or even just work with the colour that you feel is right for your intent. You can also add other items into the grid such as business cards, photos or items of jewellery. You can add more than one ring of stones around your centre stone; each new layer will increase and amplify energies. Go with your intuition, what stones you have and the amount of space you have to work with. I recommend you put your grid in a safe place where it won't be disturbed by pets or small children. You may only feel that the grid needs to be left up for an hour or two, you may want to leave it in place for days or weeks – getting everyone to step around a four-foot crystal grid in the centre of the living room probably isn't practical ... You might like to light candles and incense as you create the grid as well.

Once your grid is all set up you need to activate it. Some people like to use a specific crystal or metal wand to activate each stone in the grid, personally I just use a quartz crystal point, but the choice is yours as to what you use (and what you can afford) a well aimed finger works as well! Once you are all set up, take a moment to calm and centre yourself, then say out loud your intent, it might just be a statement, an affirmation or if you are poetic you could say it in verse.

As you state your intent point your activation wand/crystal or your finger at the centre stone and visualise energy coming up from the earth (or down from the sky) through your body, down your arm and out through your hand into the centre crystal (you don't need to make actual contact with the crystal) then move your wand from crystal to crystal around the grid linking the energy beam from one stone to the next repeating your intent as you go. Again, as we are working with the sun here then drawing down solar energy from that big 'ole fiery ball in the sky would be perfect.

Once you have linked all the stones take an overall look at the grid and visualise your required outcome. Then ground yourself and let the grid do its work. You should instinctively know when the grid is done and when you can dismantle it, or you may feel that it needs longer and requires recharging later, if it needs recharging just repeat the activation sequence again.

Don't ignore your grid, I am not suggesting it will need recharging every day but take some time every few days just to take notice of it and re-visualise your intent.

If you chose to place other items in your grid they will charge nicely with the energy and in the case of jewellery, for instance, can be taken out and worn, thereby carrying the energy from the grid with you.

If you have the room you can create a crystal grid large enough for you to sit in, this is wonderful for re-energising yourself. When you do take a crystal grid apart, don't forget to cleanse all the crystals you used.

Mirror Magic

I associate mirrors with both the moon and the sun, dark mirrors particularly seem to lend themselves to lunar workings, but mirrors can be used very effectively in sun magic. There is a lot of superstition about mirrors, so it will be a personal thing as to whether you choose to work with them.

A mirror can be used in direct sunlight to focus rays onto petition papers to burn them (please be careful) but by adding reflective magic and solar energy at the same time.

Small pieces of mirror can be added to spell pouches or used in spell work to provide reflection to show someone the error of their ways, to reverse magic or curses and to provide protection.

Using a mirror, you can direct sunlight to crystals and tools to boost the cleansing and purifying energy from the sun.

Sun Animals

There are some obvious animals that you would immediately associate with the sun (well I would anyway) such as the lion, the eagle and desert dwellers like lizards but there are a whole herd of sun animals that you can work with. Meditate and see what sun animal comes to you. Bring in the energy of sun animals to help with your spell working or to add fiery energy to your rituals. Be guided by your own intuition (as always) but here are some suggestions for sun and fire animals.

Bear

Bear plays a big part in a lot of cultures including Native American and the Celtic tradition bringing power and protection with it. Don't ever mess with a mama bear who is looking after her babies. Bear hibernates in the winter so may bring a quieter energy during those months but in spring she brings the magic of new opportunities and possibilities. Her hibernation cycle allows us to do a lot of inner work and self-reflection, but it also gives us the ability to know when the time is right and which direction we need to head off in. She brings not only the energy of the sun but also the moon along with heap loads of intuition too. Bear can be quick to react and has a bit of a temper and a tendency to be a grumpy 'ole bear at times.

Keywords: Interactions, inner knowledge, introspection, intuition, dreamtime, renewal, moon and sun magic, opportunities, fearlessness and protection.

Bee

Without these little critters whizzing about in their stripy pyjamas we would have no food … they are incredibly important. They are a representation of birth, death and rebirth and have been worshipped and honoured in many cultures for thousands of years. Often mentioned in myths and folklore is the belief that bees are the souls of those that were worthy to come back to earth.

Bees should also be told all the local gossip especially regarding births, deaths and wedding plans ... they need to know this stuff. Bees remind us to take the good stuff from life and to literally make hay (or honey) while the sun shines. Bee tells us to follow our dreams but also with a reminder to plan and save for the future too.

Keywords: Prosperity, good fortune, communication, gossip, reincarnation, goals, celebration, community, achieving your dreams, productivity, co-operation and focus.

Beetle

Beetles come in all shapes and sizes (like humans really) and bring transformation, metamorphosis and rebirth of ideas, thoughts, spirituality and complete lives. Beetles work in harmony with their surroundings and can teach us to do the same, throwing in the ability to use our intuition too. Beetles are also persistent and strong.

Keywords: Transformation, rebirth, spirituality, harmony, intuition, strength and persistence.

Cockerel

The cockerel is often linked to the Underworld and a guardian, but also another one for sacrifice. Said to not only predict the weather but also to use his power of psychic abilities to warn of impending danger. This feathered fowl likes to strut his funky stuff, he is all about sexuality and fertilisation, after all he usually has an entire hen house of chickens to service ... with his early rising and crowing about the sun rising, he is also linked to renewal and rebirth. The cockerel (or rooster) also appears in the Chinese zodiac and brings humour, eccentricity and enthusiasm.

Keywords: Sexuality, psychic abilities, sacrifice, fertility, renewal, humour, eccentricity and enthusiasm.

Cricket

The most noticeable thing about a cricket is the sound it makes, a loud noise for such a small creature. Some myths tell that crickets sing as a warning when danger is around so this little guy brings protection with it. Their song also calls to attract a mate, so it carries that love thing with it as well. The cricket song is one of relaxation, innocence and just enjoying being in the moment, take a step back from the hustle and bustle of life and be still. The cricket is a very wise 'ole chap and his knowledge is old and deep.

Keywords: Patience, luck, protection, contemplation, attraction, desires, sensitivity, innocence, relaxation, going with the flow and happiness.

Eagle

The mighty eagle immediately makes you sit up straight and take notice; he is a bird of immense power, courage, majesty and authority. As he flies through the skies he helps us to raise our vibrations and our expectations to see things from a higher view point, he guides us to inspect every aspect of our own world so that we can achieve our goals.

Keywords: Strength, courage, wisdom, knowledge, hidden truths, perspective, spiritual direction and goals.

Griffin

With the head, wings and claws of an eagle at the front and the body and tail of a lion, this animal may come across as being a bit confused. What he actually brings is protection, guardianship and retribution where needed. He is incredibly powerful and full of all things magical. His hearing is excellent, and he listens not only to what people are saying out loud but the inner thoughts as well. He symbolises the sun and the elements of both earth and air. His pathway is one of spiritual enlightenment.

Keywords: Spiritual wisdom, enlightenment, guidance, guardian, protection, vengeance, power, magic and listening.

Hawk

Hawk is a very strong personality; you will definitely know he is present. He is going to grab your attention and make you sit up and take notice. Hawk is used a lot in falconry because of his intelligence and sharp eyesight but also his seeming willingness to work together with humans. His sense of attention reminds us to stay focused on what we are supposed to be doing and not get distracted … ooh look shiny things … He also has a long history of stories telling how the hawk carries souls to the Otherworld and in tandem with those myths he is linked to quite a few different deities. Hawk sees things, perhaps that others might miss; he is incredibly honest and perceptive.

Keywords: Attention, protection, power, energy, vision, rebirth, strategy, teamwork, honesty, intelligence, respect and focus.

Hedgehog

Often associated with the world of Fairy, in fact sometimes suggested that the hedgehog is a fairy or even a witch in disguise … Linked with witchcraft the hedgehog has good and bad folklore superstitions. Hedgehogs are mostly active at dawn and dusk, the in-between times, so they have links to the Otherworld, prophecy and psychic abilities. The hedgehog is probably best known for its defence mechanism of rolling into a ball to present its sharp spines to the world, keeping it safe from predators, reflecting the ability to deal with challenges calmly and effectively. Definitely an earth element creature, the hedgehog brings a huge pack of earth magic along with abundance and fertility.

Keywords: Fairy, witchcraft, psychic abilities, prophecy, Otherworld, defence, challenges, calm, earth magic, abundance and fertility.

Horse

The horse seems to have devoted a huge part of its existence to serving mankind (thank you horseys). It works hard, carries, transports and is a companion – even the power of our cars is still measured in horse power. The horse shoe can be seen on many buildings, hung as a symbol of prosperity and good luck. There are several horse symbols carved into hillsides across the UK all of which are associated with fertility. Horses have also played a very important part in many wars throughout the ages bringing their power and strength with them. Hobby horses have also appeared in our history linked again with fertility and to ensure abundance of the crops.

Keywords: Friendship, faithfulness, freedom, endurance, power, energy, travel, loyalty, overcoming obstacles, fertility and strength.

Ladybird/ladybug

Called a ladybird in the UK and ladybug in the US, this tiny little pretty-coloured insect is a powerful animal spirit guide. The shell keeps it protected, the wings allow it to fly and they have amazing instincts, feeling vibrations through their legs to allow them to sense the energy of whatever they are touching. Their bright colours also serve as a warning to predators to keep away, guiding us to send out the same message to our enemies. The colours of this little bug also bring happiness and joy and remind us to let go of fears and live life to the fullest. The ladybird asks us to trust and have faith, not just in ourselves but in those around us too. Ladybird also brings a connection to our past lives, death and rebirth, renewal and spiritual enlightenment.

Keywords: Trust, faith, wishes, luck, protection, happiness, intuition, defence, past lives, cycle of life and enlightenment.

Lion

This has to be one of the most popular animal guides linked to courage and strength ... rawr! Lions live in family groups (prides) and share the hunting duties; essentially, they are quite laid back about life in general. Male lions are associated with the solar gods, lionesses are associated with the mother goddesses including maternity and vengeance.

Keywords: Sun magic, goddess magic, hunt, community, sharing, protection, strength, courage, co-operation, maternity, vengeance, being heard, relaxation, family and stress release.

Lizard

Lizards like the best of both worlds, in that they love to bask in the sun but also to swim in the water and they have their own in-built heat regulator as they are cold blooded. If their tail should happen to be lost (careless) it will re-grow. In ancient myths they symbolise wisdom and good fortune but also death and rebirth.

Keywords: Facing your fears, guidance, balance, re-birth, wisdom, good fortune and the cycle of life.

Peacock

The male peacock likes to strut his funky stuff and with a beautiful tail full of feathers, wouldn't you too? He brings heap loads of self-esteem, nobility, vitality and the ability to walk tall and stand proud. Peacock also brings benevolence, patience, kindness, compassion and good luck. In complete opposition to the peacock's beautiful appearance, it cannot sing to save its life, instead its shrieks are said to be the sound of the Underworld ... guess you can't have everything in life. The feathers bring a mixed message, some say to have the feathers in your home brings unhappiness, but others believe the feather is one of protection against evil and negativity ... go with your intuition on this one.

Keywords: Dignity, self-esteem, confidence, protection, patience, kindness, compassion, luck, Underworld and nobility.

Pheasant

Let's look at the male pheasant because he is basically a majestic show off, anything fancy in order to attract the ladies. Apparently, it works very well. He is all about the law of attraction, love, passion and sexuality with a bit of creativity thrown in for good measure. He knows what he wants from life and exactly how to get it. Pheasant says be your own true fabulous self. Let go and release that passion and express yourself freely. Just remember to keep a bit of balance in your life because being a total exhibitionist the whole time can be overwhelming.

Keywords: Balance, protection, creativity, sexuality, passion, attraction, judgement and being genuine.

Phoenix

You couldn't get much fierier than this beastie. A bird that lives and then dies in flame, only to be reborn again from the ashes. So obviously it is a key symbol for rebirth, shaking off that which held you back or kicked you when you were down and rising majestically from the debris. The phoenix is a bright fiery feather ball full of kick-butt transformation. Find your balance, seek clarity and take on the challenges that lie before you.

Keywords: Renewal, overcoming darkness, challenges, power, success, life, time, magic, purity, clarity, rebirth, longevity, creativity, protection, immortality, balance and transformation.

Praying mantis

This is a very quiet and peaceful creature who often appears when life is in absolute chaos. She reminds us to stop and be still, to allow ourselves to centre and focus on what is important. Allow yourself time to prioritise. This little lady thinks deeply and considers all angles before making her final decision; she takes her time before taking any steps. But let's not forget that she has a dark side, often devouring her mate when she is done with him, showing the opposite of serenity. Apparently, this is her reaction only if she feels her young are being threatened or when she is starving hungry, just a light snack? She is sharp and swift, though, decapitating his head first ...

Keywords: Balance, patience, intuition, meditation, potential, calm, aware, creativity and being mindful.

Ram

Ram is the symbol of Aries and as such he represents leadership and authority. He is also a rather fiery and virile character with a bit of a temper on occasion. He also associates with a lot of ancient gods particularly those that were powerful leaders. The ram often lives in harsh conditions but deals with them in his stride. He is known to literally butt heads to fight for what he believes in or what he wants. He certainly carries a lot of stamina, power and force with him.

Keywords: Protection, no fear, leadership, energy, force, power, stubborn and virility.

Salamander

Well this little guy is full of fire energy ... and water. He is always slotted into the solar animal category but, actually, he loves the water. He brings the characteristics of both elements. He also likes to come out at dusk to hunt for his food, so he has a balance in life that we should pay attention to, making the best of what is available to him. If he should happen to lose his tail (careless) it regrows (clever) representing to us the ability of rebirth and renewal (thankfully we don't have tails ... anymore). He adjusts and adapts to his surroundings and takes notice of any changes in his area. He actually packs a huge bag of correspondences and can provide support in a whole range of areas.

Keywords: Energy, growth, balance, transformation, spirituality, adapting, opportunity, resources, emotions, secrets and clarity.

Scorpion

Scorpion is a solitary creature who prefers his own company although he does like the occasional passionate, controlling sexual fling. The life of a scorpion is definitely one of intense short-lived passion followed by longer bouts of self-imposed (and preferred) solitude. Defence, control and protection are keywords here. A sun-filled creature that has a definite sting in its tail, Scorpion can also be scared of feeling vulnerable. It looks a bit dismal at first but if scorpion has come to you, have a look at the areas of your life that it might reflect ...

Keywords: Transition, sex, control, solitude, passion, protection, defence and vulnerability.

Snake

Quite often a shadow guide, the snake has so many wonderful qualities that will help and guide you. It sheds its skin which reminds us that we can shed our illusions and any self-imposed limitations or ideas and brings a link to astral travel. Snake also brings fertility, creation and transformation. He is also seen as a symbol of sexuality and linked with many deities for that same reason. Snake is energy, raw power and our inner spark of spirituality but he also brings healing and wisdom.

Keywords: Transformation, fertility, astral travel, creativity, sexuality, power, spirituality and healing, wisdom.

Spider

Another creature that a lot of people are afraid of but really they are incredibly magical and have a lot to teach us. They weave the web of fate and bring a balance between the past and future bringing spirituality and creativity. Spider brings awareness of your own web of life and how you create and design everything that happens around you. Spider hands back the responsibility of creating your own environment to you, with a reminder that YOU are in charge.

Keywords: Creation, weaving reality, infinity, balance, past/present/future, responsibility and spirituality.

Swan

Beautiful graceful creatures that bring inner beauty, self-esteem and innocence as they glide along the surface of the water. Swan is also associated with love, poetry and music and is often referred to in myths as representing the soul of a person. It is also worth looking at the story of the ugly duckling, the baby bird that others rejected and ridiculed who grew up to be a beautiful swan. Swan also brings the ability to tap into your intuition and psychic abilities bringing about altered states of awareness. Swan teaches us to go with the flow and accept that which we cannot change. Swans also mate for life and are dedicated to their partners making a commitment that is bonding.

Keywords: Beauty, self-esteem, love, the arts, inspiration, inner self, intuition, psychic abilities, going with the flow, acceptance, dedication, commitment and respect.

Some of these meanings have been taken from my book *Pagan Portals Animal Magic*.

Meditation to Meet a Solar Animal

Make yourself comfortable in a place where you won't be disturbed.

Close your eyes and focus on your breathing, deep breaths in ... deep breaths out ...

As your world around you dissipates, you find yourself standing on a seashore, the sky above you is a clear blue and the sun is shining. It is not too hot, but a pleasant heat and the warm sun touches your skin.

You are standing on soft white sand, so you take your shoes off and wriggle your toes.

To your left is the ocean with the waves lapping gently on the shore. In front of you are mountains.

There is a light breeze and as you turn to your right you see sand dunes with clusters of tall grasses waving and bobbing around in the wind.

Beyond the sand dunes you can just see the tops of lush green trees, what looks to be a forest.

Sit down on the sand and just be still for a moment. Listen to the sounds around you, feel the sun and the breeze on your skin. What do you hear? What can you feel? What do you see?

Set the focus and intent that you would like to meet a solar animal ... whether you ask silently in your head or say it out loud ...

Be still and see what animal appears to you, look to the skies, the water, the sand dunes or beyond from the forest ... what animal comes to you?

Be patient ... and when an animal presents itself let it come to you. If you have any questions, ask the animal and listen to the response.

Take note of the animal's characteristics, what is it? What colourings or markings does it have?

Once you have finished communing with the animal, thank it for its time and guidance.

Know that this place is always here if you want to come back.

Stand back up and dust yourself down.

Take a last look around you and then slowly and gently come back to this reality.

Note down anything the animal said to you and what it looked like.

Also do some research as to what the animal means and what its characteristics are and how they relate to you and situations in your life at the moment. It may be part of the message.

Solar Deities

What makes a deity a solar one? Well …now that is a good question and I actually think it is up to you (see how I can so easily pass the buck).

I have listed below those deities that are often associated with the sun, either because they were worshipped as a sun deity or because they have developed correspondences with the sun over time.

At the end of the day (that would be sunset …) it is entirely up to you who you choose to work with for sun magic or indeed if you decide to work with a deity at all – absolutely your call.

However, I would advise, before you go leaping into a ritual or any magic and just picking a deity at random … do your homework first. Research, read up, learn about and generally get the low down on any deity before you decide to work with them. I cannot be held responsible for you being struck down by the fury of the gods because you didn't research properly … honour and respect above all else.

Adonis

A god of beauty and desire and apparently a bit of a looker. Adonis was born to Myrrha who had unfortunately been turned into a myrrh tree at the time. Later on, Aphrodite fell in love with him and Persephone looked after him, they fought about it and Zeus had to step in and settle the argument. In the end Adonis chose to be with Aphrodite for two thirds of the year and Persephone for a third. Adonis eventually died after being attacked by a wild boar sent by Artemis because she was jealous of his hunting skills. Although some stories tell that Ares the god of war sent the boar because he was sleeping with Aphrodite too. When Adonis died, Aphrodite let nectar flow over his blood and the flower anemone grew in its place.

Aine

A Celtic goddess of love, wealth, sovereignty and the summer, she is also a goddess of the earth and nature. Said to be the daughter of Eogabail (try pronouncing that one), who was a member of the Tuatha De Danann. She was also believed to have married the sea god Manannan Mac Lir. Aine is often described as being a Fairy Queen. Some believe her to be a Lady of the Lake. She brings luck and good magic to those that follow her. Seems she was a bit of a floozy, bedding many human men and bearing their children.

Agni

A Hindu god of fire. Agni looks after and protects the home. He covers various aspects of fire including domestic and sacred fire, lightning and the sun. Fire is often used in many Hindu ceremonies. Agni is usually depicted with flaming red hair and riding a goat. Agni is the son of the Celestial Waters, fire being carried down to earth with the rain and then drawn up through the vegetation that grows.

Akycha

A solar goddess from Alaska worshipped from Inuit mythology. She once lived upon the earth but fled to the skies after her brother raped her.

Alaunus

A Celtic deity of healing and prophecy, he brings harmony, honesty and abundance. I suspect the link to the sun comes from him being a very nurturing god.

Amaterasu

Her parents Izanami and Izanagi made their daughter ruler of the skies and she is seen in the Shinto religion as the sun goddess, the most important deity and ruler of the Takama no Hara (the

High Celestial Plain) so this girl has a lot of clout. Her sister is Susanoo the storm goddess. In art she is often depicted sitting down back to back with her brother Tsukiyomi-no-Mikoto, the moon god. Cockerels are associated with her as they shout about the rising son and the raven is believed to be her messenger. Her symbol is an octagonal mirror.

Amun

A very important and powerful god from ancient Egypt he was named 'King of the Gods'. His name translates as 'the hidden one' and his image was often painted in blue to symbolise invisibility. He was noted as a god for those that were oppressed. He is often associated with the god Ra (or Re) and Ptah as part of a triad; sometimes seen as a single god with all other deities as his manifestations. He is often depicted with a human body and the head of a ram. When associated with the sun god Ra/Re, he is sometimes seen as part of another triad, the Theban triad which includes Mut and Khons.

Ao

A Maori god, Ao is the god of light, a primordial god of nature and the world of the living. He is associated with Ata the god of morning and Whaitua the god of space. Ao fights against the dark forces.

Apollo

An Olympian god of music, song, poetry, healing, disease, prophecy and looking after children. He was often depicted with long hair and with very handsome features. He carries a branch of laurel, a bow and arrow, a lyre and is often seen with a raven.

Anyanwu

An Igbo deity thought to live within the sun. He is one of the main spirits of the Igbo. He is seen as a perfect image of a human.

Arinnitti

A Hittite goddess of the sun who provided protection from war and disaster. She was one of the principal deities of the Hittite empire and the monarchy. She brought judgement of the righteous kind, mercy and authority.

Aryaman

His name translates as 'the bright sunlight behind God' and he is one of the earlier Devas or Vedic deities in the Hindu culture. Aryaman symbolises the sun's energy, he controls the movement of time. Aryaman is often invoked to witness Hindu marriage vows.

Atanua

A Polynesian dawn goddess of the oceans, from the Marquesas. Her creations were made with the aid of her amniotic fluid (resourceful).

Atarapa

Polynesian goddess of the dawn. There seem to be several goddesses for different stages of dawn break. Atarapa is the first created being.

Aten

Aten was given the job of principle god of Egypt during the reign of Akhenaten. He wasn't a new god but was a relatively unknown aspect of the sun god. Aten is the traditional name for the sun disc itself. He was considered to be an aspect of Ra-Amun-Horus. Ra represented the day, Amun the sun in the Underworld and Horus the sunrise. So, Aten became the visible sun, the source of all life and the sole deity.

Atum

A solar creator god from ancient Egypt, he was created from the primordial waters and carried both sexes within him ...or her ... His name is derived from the word 'tem' meaning 'complete'. He was the first god in the Ennead of Heliopolis, a collection of nine deities. He is often depicted as wearing a king's crown. He is another god that later became associated or combined with Ra, known as Atum-Ra; the sun god, Atum Khepri; the rising sun god and Atum Horus; the solar god. Atum was believed to carry all of their characteristics.

Aurora

Roman goddess of the dawn, the Greeks called her Eos. She was daughter of the Titans, Hyperion and Theia and the sister of Helios the sun god and Selene the moon goddess. She rose from the sea every morning and took a ride across the sky just ahead of the sun, in her horse-drawn chariot. She carried with her a pitcher filled with dew that she sprinkled onto the earth.

Baldr

One of the Norse Aesir gods, he is the son of Odin and Frigg. A handsome and happy chap, in fact so glorious that he gives off a bright light. It is believed he was the divine force behind all life.

Bast or Bastet

Egyptian goddess who covers the home, women, cats, fertility and childbirth. She also protects against diseases and acts as a guide to the dead in the afterlife. Her father was the sun god Ra and she is often associated with the all-seeing Eye of Ra.

Belanos/Belenos/Belia Mawr

A Celtic god of the sun whose powers brought solar healing. He is sometimes depicted riding a horse, throwing thunder bolts and using his radiating wheel as a shield.

Beiwe/Beivai/Paive

A Sami (from the Artic region) goddess, the name is literally given to the sun itself as they believe the sun to be a goddess. She looks after their herds, their food and their bodies. Her symbol is a spinning wheel and offerings of flax and a rich porridge are made to her.

Dagr/Dagur

In old Norse the name translates as 'day'. Dagr, god in his personification of the day time. His parents are Nott the giantess goddess of the night and her third husband Delling (meaning dawn).

Dažbog

A Slavic sun and fire god. His father was Svarog, a god of blacksmiths. His name translates as 'giving god'. He is the patron of the hearth, fire and rain. In some Slovenian translations of Greek texts, the name Helios was translated as Dazbog.

Ekhi

The goddess Ekhi hales from Basque mythology and she is the goddess of the sun, one who protects humanity. She destroys evil and apparently protects against spirits of the night and ... witches. Oooer! She is saluted at sunset when she sinks into the womb of her mother, Earth, to rise again the next morning.

Eos

Greek goddess of the dawn and one of the Titan gods. She rose up into the sky from the river Okeanos at the beginning of each day dispelling the mists of the night. She is often seen driving a chariot drawn by winged horses or sometimes flying herself with her own set of wings. Her brother is Helios the sun god and her sister Selene the moon goddess. She is believed to have had a bit of an eye for the gentlemen, well more than an eye ...

Étaín

A Celtic goddess whose name translates as 'shining one'. She is a goddess of grace and beauty. She is associated with the sun, the dawn, the sea, water, transformation, healing, medicine, music and fertility. Flowers are said to bloom when she is near.

Freyr

An Old Norse god from the Vanir tribe of deities. Also, an honorary member of the Aesir. He was said to be loved by all and hated by none. He controlled harvests, wealth, fertility, peace, health and abundance so it stands to reason that everyone wanted to keep on his good side! He owned a ship that could be folded up and carried in a small bag (seriously he would make a fortune with that idea). When on land he travels in a chariot drawn by boars.

Guaraci

Guaraci is from Guarani mythology and is the god of the sun, he who created all living creatures. He was a twin with his sister Jaci who was the goddess of the moon. They were the first gods created by Tupa, the god of thunder.

Gun Ana

Turkish, Hungarian and Kazakhstan solar goddess. The name 'gun' translates as the name for the sun. A powerful goddess of life, fertility, heat and health. She lives on the seventh floor of the sky. The rays from the sun are thought to be the strings between the sun and the spirits of all living things. Her image is often depicted with glowing yellow skin. Gun Ana (the sun) and Ay Ata (the moon) were husband and wife.

Helios

Greek Titan god of the sun, the god of sight and guardian of oaths. Helios lived in a golden palace on the river Okeanos at the ends of the earth. He rose each dawn, crowed with light and drove his chariot pulled by winged horses. When he reached Hesperides in the far west he descended into the golden cup which took him through the Okeanos back to his starting point in the east. He is often shown as a handsome chap wearing purple robes with a crown of sunlight.

Hors

Slavic god of the old sun which dies at the winter solstice. He moved across the sky during the day but underground during the night. His name literally translates as 'sun'.

Horus

A god from ancient Egypt, he often appeared in the form of a falcon, his right eye was said to be the sun representing power and his left eye was the moon, that represented healing. He appears under different names such as Horus in the horizon (Haremakhet) and Horus, son of Isis (Harsiese). He is another deity associated closely with the sun god Ra/Re. Sometimes Horus is shown as a winged sun disk.

Huitzilopochtli

Whilst the name looks like I sat on the keyboard ... he is actually an Aztec sun and war god; often portrayed as a hummingbird or an eagle in artwork. His brothers are the stars and his sister is the moon. He guided the migration of Aztecs from Aztlan to their home in the Valley of Mexico. The Aztecs believed that their sun god required daily offerings of human blood and hearts. The sacrificial hearts were offered to the sun god then burnt.

Hunahpu

This Mayan god started his career in the Underworld but was then promoted to become god of the sun along with his twin brother Xbalanque, who became god of the moon.

Hyperion

Son of Uranus (heaven) and Gaia (earth), Hyperion is a Greek Titan god of heavenly light. His wife Theia is lady of the shining blue sky. His name translates as 'watcher from above'. He is father of the sun and dawn.

Inti

Thought to be the ancestor of all Incas, Inti was god of the sun; shown in human form but with a face of a golden disk with rays of light and flames extending outwards. His sister, Mama-Quilla, was the moon goddess.

Khepri

An Egyptian god of creation, rebirth and movement of the sun. Khepri's name translates as 'he who is coming into being' and he was often depicted with the body of a man and the head of a scarab beetle. (Not the most attractive look.) He is sometime associated with the god Atrum and also the god Ra/Re.

Kinich Ahau

A Mayan god in charge of the sun. He controls disease and drought. His images often depict him with a hooked nose, eyes that are just crosses and a beard with curls at the corners of his mouth. He was the sun and thought to turn into a jaguar each night.

Koyash

A sun god from Turkic mythology. He is often seen as a winged horse or a fiery bird. Koyash can create solar strands from his hands to burn his victims if he chooses. He is a provider of light and growth but also seen as a warrior. His father was the sky god and his mother the earth goddess.

Malakbel

A West Semitic sun and messenger god, he was worshipped in the ancient city of Palmyra, although his name may have Babylonian origins. A marble altar from Palmyra has engravings showing the sequence of the sun throughout the year. He is often seen depicted alongside Ablibol, the moon god.

Malina

A solar goddess from the Inuit religion, she is often linked with her brother, Anningan the lunar god. She is always running away from him across the sky after an argument.

Marici

A Buddhist and Taoist goddess, she is sometimes seen with three eyes in four heads, the left head being that of a pig. She has four arms on each side of her body. In her hands she holds a sun, moon, bell, golden seal and halberd (a spear and battle axe). She rides a chariot pulled by seven boars. She is worshipped as a goddess of light and a guardian of all people.

Nahundi

Ancient sun and law god from Persia. Not much known about him other than his name translates as 'creator of the day'.

Nanahuatzin

An Aztec deity, he sacrificed himself in fire so that he could continue with his role as the sun and shine his light on the Earth. His names translates as 'full of sores' ewwwww.

Neaera

Neaera (Neaira) was a nymph who was loved by the sun god Helios, she gave him two children, both daughters. Her name translates as 'new rising', possibly indicating her role as a goddess of the dawn.

Nefertem

An Egyptian god of the lotus blossom. Some suggestions have been made that he was an aspect of Atum. Atum represented the sun so Nerfertem was considered the god of the sunrise. It was believed that he was born every sunrise and as the day progressed he turned into Atum before dying with the sunset. Starting the same cycle again the next day.

Olwen

A Welsh goddess, the meaning of her name has been suggested as being 'the golden wheel' but in other sources as 'white track'. Wherever she walked, trefoil plants would appear. She appears to be linked to the fairy world and also as the role of May Queen.

Ra/Re

Possibly one of the most well-known sun gods. He was the primary sun god of ancient Egypt and said to be King of the Gods (see the part about Amun). He was powerful and the creator of all things. Solar temples were thought to have been built in his honour. Many of the tombs in the Valley of the Kings include depictions of Ra and his journey through the Underworld, which took twelve 'stages'. It was believed that Ra was swallowed every evening by the goddess Nut as the sun went down; he then travelled through the world overnight and was reborn again the next morning.

Saranyu

Hindu goddess of the dawn and the clouds. She was the first wife of Surya, the sun god.

Saulė

A Baltic sun goddess who brought energy and regeneration to the planet and all life upon it. She rode on her horse-drawn sky chariot, with its copper wheels each day, washing them in the sea in the evening, then heading into her castle at the end of the day.

Savitr

A Hindu Vedic deity seen with golden eyes, hands and tongue. His hair is also yellow, and he wears yellow clothes. He is carried in a golden chariot drawn by two horses. Some categorise him as a god of the sunrise and sunset. He is a protector and a visionary and supports the sky.

Sekhmet

One of the oldest known Egyptian goddesses, her name means 'power'. She is seen with the body of a woman and the head of a lion. Sometimes she also wears a sun disc on her head (looks uncomfortable). When seated in her pictures she holds the ankh of life, when standing she holds a sceptre made from papyrus. She carries the title of 'destroyer' associated with Ptah the creator and Nefertum the healer. Her representation was the midday sun which showed her as destruction, on the positive side this could remove plagues and disease. She is the patron of healers. She is bringer of pestilence but also healer.

Shamash (Utu in Sumaria)

The god of the sun in the Mesopotamian religion, he formed a triad of astral deities with the moon god Sin (Sumerian Nanna) and the goddess of Venus, Ishtar (Sumerian Inanna). He brought light to the darkness and overcame evil. He was a god of justice to men during the day and judge to the Underworld during the night.

Shapash

A Mesopotamian sun goddess often referred to as 'torch of the gods'. She sees all, leads souls into the Underworld, has power over all the lands and crops and acts as a messenger.

Sol

The name says it all! A Roman sun god often appearing with the moon goddess, Luna. He began as Sol Indiges, disappeared for a while and was reintroduced later as Sol Invictus which translates as 'unconquered sun'. Sol Indiges was an early god from around 79 CE. Sol Invictus appears around 724 CE. Sol Invictus is linked with December 25 and Christmas Day, the story says that Sol died for three days and was reborn on 25 December ...

Sopdu

An Egyptian solar god but also a god of war associated with the east and referred to as 'Lord of the East'. He represented the sun as it rises in the east and the heat of the midday sun. His name in hieroglyphs was a thorn symbol which translates as 'skilled man' or 'sharp ones'. The symbol was referred to by the Egyptians as 'the tooth'.

Sulis

An ancient British healing goddess but also a solar and fertility deity. Her shrine was in the city of Bath, Somerset. Her name may have derived from the Celtic word 'sul' meaning 'sun' and 'eye'. Fires were kept burning at her shrine where there are natural hot springs. When the Romans arrived they renamed her Minerva Medica, but also as Sulis Minerva. Symbols on her shrine include antlers to represent the rays of the sun and eyes to symbolise the sun.

Surya

In Hinduism this deity plays both the role of a sun god and the sun itself. He is often invoked at dawn on a daily basis. He can heal, cure disease, dispel evil and darkness and illuminates the world. He is also another deity that rides across the skies in a horse-drawn chariot, his head surrounded by rays of light.

Tama-nui-te-rā

A Maori god of the sun. A Maui caught him in a snare and beat him so that he would travel across the sky at a slower pace.

Theia

A Greek Titan goddess of sight and the shining blue sky. She is associated with silver and gold. She had three children; Helios the sun, Eos the dawn and Selene the moon. Her name translates as 'sight prophesy'.

Thesan

An Etruscan sky goddess of the dawn but also of childbirth, love and divination. She sports an impressive pair of wings on her back. Her names translates as 'dawn'. She illuminates the dark, throws light onto the future and allows us to see clearly.

Tonatiuh

An Aztec sun god of the fifth and final era. He was a god constantly threatened by his birth at sunrise and his death at the end of the day, his journey across the sky taking enormous effort. He is depicted at the centre of the Aztec calendar with an eagle's claw holding human hearts.

Ushas

A Hindu goddess of the dawn, she keeps away the evil spirits of the night. She wears a gold veil and red robes bringing light to the world. During the day she rides her golden chariot (seriously where do they get all these chariots from?) across the sky.

Wuriupranili

An Australian aboriginal sun goddess. Each morning she lights a torch made out of bark and travels across the sky from east to west then at the end of the day puts the torch out in the water using the glowing embers to guide her beneath the earth.

Xihe

A solar goddess from China. She is believed to have invented the calendar and is mother of ten suns, which are in the form of three-legged birds. Each day one of the sun birds travels around the world on a carriage driven by her.

Yhi

Sun goddess from Australia, she is said to have created all the plants and animals including humans.

Meditation to Meet a Sun Deity

Make yourself comfortable in a place where you won't be disturbed.

Close your eyes and focus on your breathing, deep breaths in ...deep breaths out ...

As your world around you dissipates you find yourself in a temple, tall bleached white stone pillars surround you with a beautiful mosaic floor beneath your feet, sparkling with the colours of the rainbow.

You look up and realise the top of the temple is open to the sky which is a bright azure blue and the sun is shining brightly.

The walls are decorated with gold and bronze sun symbols and disks of shining metal which reflect the rays of sunshine.

There are stone benches around the edges of the temple and as you investigate, you find that one end of the temple appears to be an altar.

You make your way over to the altar and notice that in the centre is a large candle with the flame burning brightly. To each side are smaller tealight candles, most of them are already lit, but one is sitting unlit ready for you, so you take it and light it from the centre flame and set it down with the others.

Also, on the altar are dishes of incense burning, the smoke fills the air with a delicious and heady scent.

To one side are large cushions, so you pick one up and bring it to the centre in front of the altar and place it on the floor, then you seat yourself comfortably on it.

A slight breeze comes across the temple and brings with it a shower of blossom petals from the trees just outside.

You sit and watch the flames from the candles, breathing in the incense fragrance. As you sit quietly contemplating, a figure catches your eye. A person enters the temple and comes to stand next to you.

They ask permission to sit beside you ...

Talk to them, ask them questions, tell them what you seek ...

Listen to the reply ...

When you are finished they get up to leave, but just before doing so they put something in your hand, a gift for you.

You thank them for the gift and their time and guidance.

Continue to sit here for as long as you want, know that this place is here if you ever want to return.

When you are ready, slowly and gently come back to this reality.

Make a note of the person's characteristics, what they looked like and what wisdom they shared with you. What gift did they leave you and what does it mean to you?

Note: Be open to whatever god or goddess comes to you in your meditations. Just because you sit down to work with a solar deity, it might not be who (or what) arrives. Trust that deity, spirit and the universe know better, if someone unexpected arrives, go with it. Find out why they are there and what they can do to assist you. As an example, when I tested the meditation above, I expected to be met by a solar deity, but that wasn't who arrived. What I got was a visit from a being who told me he was an ancient Dali Lama … but if you think about it, he wears lively solar colours and spends his life living in the brightness of the sun. He was also very honest and gave me some incredible insights.

Sun Invocations

An invocation means to invoke someone or something, i.e. to invoke a deity. It is the act of referring to deity to ask for their help or support. It can also be in the form of a blessing.

You could use an invocation to ask for help from a deity but also to gain support or energy from the sun. (Or the moon or any planet.)

Using invocations when you are asking for help or guidance, when you are in ritual or working spells is a great way to boost your magic. But also remember to give thanks afterwards either in the form of actually saying thank you or making an offering, or better still ... both.

For the sun you could use:

Great sun, giver of all life
Lend me your fiery power and energy this day
Fill me with your magic and might
So that joy and happiness may complete my plight

It doesn't have to rhyme! I am not just saying that because poetry is not my thing, it really doesn't have to be perfect, it just needs to be honest and from the heart.

If you are writing an invocation to a sun deity or any deity for that matter, do some research first, find out all you can about them and make sure your words are suitable and correspond not only to your requirement but also to the deity concerned. Be respectful at all times.

Drawing Down the Sun

Stand outside in the sunshine, at the time of day of your choosing. Make yourself comfortable with your arms thrown open wide. Allow the energy and warmth of the sun to enter your body, filling you with energy. Either feel the energy entering your body through your hands and running through your veins to every body part or visualise breathing in the sun energy through your mouth. When you feel that you are finished, remember to thank the sun.

This is my version of a chant/poem to recite when drawing down the sun:

God of the sun, you have many names in many cultures across time.
You are a constant source of life, energy and passion.
In the heat of the day we ask you to shine your light upon us.
Honour us by joining with us and allow us to feel your presence
within our heart and soul.

Move your feet apart and raise your arms to welcome the sun.
When you feel the sun's energy and the presence of his spirit:

I am the father of all life
I am the passion of living
The flames of growth
The spark of creation in the earth
I am the sparkle of light on the water.

Whenever you have need during the daylight hours
Any day of the week
Look up to the skies and feel my heat
I am the spirit within you.

Whether on your own or gathered as a group
Look to me, learn from me
And honour my wisdom
I will share my knowledge, passion and strength.

Celebrate under the sky
Dance in the light of my rays
Eat, drink, sing and make merry
All in honour of my name.

I am the spirit of passion and love for the earth
Share my love and joy to all beings
Strive towards your goals
Keep your faith strong
Love and respect one another.

My power and might will open doors for you
I will shine the light to guide your way
My spirit and energy will fill you with the power
And desire to keep you on the right pathway.

Sun Ritual

This ritual was written by our lovely Kitchen Witch ritual team, huge thanks to Ness, Sue, Josh, Gwyneth and Heather for allowing me to share it here. It is written for a group but could easily be adapted for solitary use.

Four element callers form a doorway from the east into the circle, holding smudge sticks made from rosemary and cinnamon to waft over each person as they enter the circle.

Cast the circle:

Cast this circle round and right
Rays of light to keep things bright
With the power and spirit of the fiery sun
The casting of this sun magic circle is done.

East:

Guardian of the east, element of air, you are the dawn of each new day, filled with potential and possibilities.

You are new beginnings, opportunities and promise, the connecting force that unites us with all life on earth. You are the gentle Summer breeze, that carries our wishes and prayers to the Gods.

You rule our thoughts, wisdom and intuition and bring the gift of new life and the winds of change. Air, we ask you to watch over us and protect us during our ritual. Hail and Welcome.

As the east is called each person in circle is anointed with chamomile & honey oil.

Cups of chamomile tea are passed around the circle for each person to drink.

South:

Welcome Guardians of the south, element of fire, realm of the midday sun.

At this moment you are at the pinnacle of your powers.

Firing up the energy of passion within all life.

Midday sun you transform us, with your power bringing us courage and joy for life,

as we dance within the heat from your flares, that radiate out across the universe.

We bid you hail and welcome!

As the south is called each person in circle is anointed with cinnamon oil.

Cups of cinnamon tea are passed around the circle for each person to drink.

West:

Guardians of west, element of water, home to the setting sun.

We welcome you.

As you cast across the sky bringing with you impending darkness of night,

we know that you bring the promise of a new day ahead.

At this time of quiet, we admire your beauty, taking this time to reflect on mysteries of the self, our intuition and emotions.

Hail and Welcome!

As the west is called each person in circle is anointed with orange oil.

Cups of orangeade are passed around the circle for each person to drink.

North:

Element of earth, guardian of the north-the land of the midnight sun.

You bring us the wisdom of experience, sustaining life and providing growth and abundance for our food, flowers and trees.

Yours are the mountains, caves and crystals.

The world of Fairy and the Sidhe.

In your realm of the midnight sun, the sun waits patiently as

Mother Earth turns on her axis until he is reborn – rising again in the east.

Just as we, once your arms have welcomed us into your womb of the underworld, wait to be reborn, back from the darkness, according to the cycle of life.

Element of earth, we call upon you to be present today at our ritual to sustain and nurture us.

We bid you hail and welcome!

As the north is called each person in circle is anointed with ginger oil.

Cups of ginger tea are passed around the circle for each person to drink.

Description of Ra:

In Ancient Egypt, going back 6000 years, there were only two deities. As the millennia proceeded, this pantheon grew in number, but one deity is still considered the 'Big Kahuna'. This top dog of a God is none other than Ra. He is generally a sun god but has been known to dabble as a sky god, a celestial god, king of the gods, and at the very beginning, it was said he created the entire universe.

Like many gods and goddesses, he comes in many forms; but usually he can be seen as a man, a falcon, or some sort of odd mixture of the two. But you can always spot him, as he dons a gigantic sun-like disc on his head, adorned with an Egyptian cobra, representing his divinity.

As with most cultures and beliefs, and the same goes for Egypt; the sun does not merely move itself across the sky. It is always ushered by the sun god in some sense. And Ra likes to travel by flying boat. Every morning, Ra begins his journey by being birthed from the goddess Nut. He then hops on said flying boat and makes his way across the sky, as the sun begins to grow in strength. At some point during his daily travels, he always encounters the serpent god Apophis. Apophis is the god of chaos, arch-nemesis to Ra, forever trying to destroy the order of Ra's nicely organised universe. It is said Apophis is a god of primordial evil; and although Ra destroys him every day, he never truly goes away, coming back daily for a butt-kicking. When the day is coming to an end, and the power of the sun is waning; Ra continues to travel. He and the sun are eaten by the very goddess who birthed him that morning. Once eaten, he rides his boat to the underworld, back to the darkness of earth, awaiting the dawn, so he may start all over again.

It is easy to see why Ra has remained the head honcho for so long. The sun, in all its magnificence, has always represented life to the human race. Ra has always been the god that has brought life and light, warmth and growth, ambition and passion. He has always been the VIP, sitting upon high, overlooking his creation and ensuring we survive each day.

Ra Invocation:

Almighty Ra, god of the sun, creator of all, patron of life.

We invoke you to our ritual, so we may honour all that you are.

From the soft, reviving light of dawn, to the dark anticipation of night.

You sail the skies, bestowing life upon all you touch.

Glimmers of warmth that give us hope, rays of ambition that drive us forward.

Flares of rage and waves of passion for a heart of incandescence.

Gift us the powerful energy of the sun, so we may bring life to our debilitated.

Destruction to our enemies and ascension to our spirits.

Hail and Welcome!

Mandala – ask everyone to forage in the local area for leaves, twigs and stones to create a central natural mandala in the middle of the circle.

Drumming whilst the mandala is being created.

Drawing down the sun – directing the energy into the mandala.

Make yourself comfortable with your arms thrown open wide. Allow the energy and warmth of the sun to enter your body, filling you with energy. Either feel the energy entering your body through your hands and running through your veins to every body part or visualise breathing in the sun energy through your mouth.

Quote the 'drawing down the sun' chant from this book.

Send the energy raised out into the universe to go where it is needed the most.

Thanks to Ra:

Celestial father, divine creator, Ra, we thank you.

You have bestowed upon us the power of the sun.

Our hearts are a little warmer, our spirits a little lighter.

You have brought a spark to our desires and a fire to our passions.

We may go from this circle, our souls ablaze, giving gratitude for your favour.

Hail and Farewell!

North:

Element of earth.

We thank you for your presence here today, for your nurturing and sustaining energies and for the natural world that we see all around us.

We bid you hail and farewell!

As north is being thanked, small bite-size ginger cookies are passed around for everyone to eat.

West:

Guardians of west, element of water, home to the setting sun.

We thank you for your presence here today.

We have stood in quiet contemplation and reflected on our intuition and mysteries of the self

As you disappear from our sky bringing the darkness,

We look forward to the new day ahead when again you will return.

Hail and Farewell!

As West is being thanked, small bite-size orange cookies are passed around for everyone to eat.

South:

Guardians of the south, element of fire, realm of the midday sun!
We give you thanks for being here with us today.
May your energy of passion, courage and love of life stay with us.
Hail and Farewell!

As south is being thanked, small bite-size cinnamon cookies are passed around for everyone to eat.

East:

Element of air, we thank you for your presence here today.
For bringing us new beginnings and transformation and for protecting us during our ritual.
Air, we bid you hail and farewell!

As east is being thanked, small bite-size honey cookies are passed around for everyone to eat.

Closing the circle:

As I uncast this circle round and right
Rays of light that kept things bright
With the power and spirit of the fiery sun
The uncasting of this sun magic circle is done
Merry meet, merry part, merry meet again.

Solar Plexus

There are seven main chakras, but a lot more you can investigate if working with charkas interests you. The word chakra is derived from the Sanskrit word meaning wheel. If you could see the chakras (as many psychics can) you would see a wheel of energy continuously spinning around. Some clairvoyants perceive chakras as colourful wheels or flowers with a point in the centre.

The chakras start at the base of the spine, or at a floating point between your feet and the base of your spine and finish at the top of the head. Though generally fixed in the spinal column, they can be found on both the front and back of the body, and work through it.

Each chakra vibrates or spins at a different speed. Each chakra is stimulated by its own and complementary colour, and a range of crystals for specific uses.

The main seven chakra colours are red, orange, yellow, green, blue, indigo, and violet, reflecting the colours in the rainbow, with the addition of white and brown if you work with the Soul and Earth Star chakras. The size and brightness of the wheels vary depending on experience, health and energy levels.

The energy travels between each chakra along a pathway called a meridian. There are several versions of how the energy moves between each chakra; some see it as working in a continuous circle, the energy flowing from one chakra to another flowing up through the chakras, around and back down.

Another version is that the energy flows in a criss-cross system similar to the Caduceus symbol going from one to the other crossing over as the snakes do, and another idea is that the energy flows in a spiral up and down linking each chakra.

If the chakras are not balanced, or if the energies are blocked, the energy slows down. You may feel listless, tired, out of sorts, or depressed. Not only will your physical body be affected but so will your emotional and mental state.

Having all your chakras in tip top working condition means a happy and balanced you. If the chakras are opened too much, you get an overload of energy. If the chakras are closed, the energy cannot flow properly which may also lead to illness.

Whenever a person blocks whatever experience they are having, in turn they block their chakras, which stop working properly or altogether. When the chakras are functioning properly, each will be bright, open and spinning freely.

You can use visualisation and meditate to work with your chakras; you can also aid this by working with crystals that correspond to each chakra.

I am only going to look at the solar plexus chakra here as it corresponds to sun magic, being solar. If you are interested in working with your chakras do look into it, there are plenty of resources on the net or books on the subject (I can highly recommend Elen Sentier's book *Celtic Chakras*).

The solar plexus chakra is yellow in colour and is located just above your naval and corresponds with your digestive organs. It affects your will power and your energy centre. This chakra houses your personal power, action, empowerment and your ego. This chakra is the area where responsibility for others, caring for others, personal honour and courage emerge.

Sometimes called the power chakra, the energy of this chakra is about your personal power and self-esteem, manifestation, creativity and feeling centred.

This chakra's meaning is all about the concept of 'the will'. The solar plexus chakra meanings relate to self-confidence, self-esteem, the ego, personal power, self-worth, clarity and creativity.

This chakra is responsible for the effective flow of energy not only to this region but throughout the whole body. Improving energy flow to the solar plexus may clear problems that have been producing lack and limitations.

It is also a powerful area to bring an improvement in your finances as its energy aids you to manifest money. As you improve the energy flow here, you will develop a stronger will, a clear sense of self and will improve your ability to manifest.

This is the chakra that is responsible for manifestation on all levels. Many people only think of manifestation in terms of money, but in a more spiritual sense most of us would like to manifest other things. Good health, better relationships, self-esteem, talents and abilities, your overall spirituality and health ... the list goes on.

Solar plexus correspondences

Glands and Organs: The diaphragm, the breath, adrenals, skin, digestive organs, stomach, duodenum, pancreas, gall bladder, liver.

Colour: Yellow

Gems: Citrine, gold topaz, amber, tiger eye, gold calcite, yellow jasper, sunstone

Scents: Bergamot, juniper, lavender, rosemary, black pepper, cinnamon, clove, coriander, geranium, ginger, grapefruit and vetiver

Element: Fire

Syllable for chanting: Ram or Ah

Yoga Posture: Dhanaurasana – Bow Pose

Balanced energy: Outgoing and Confident, self-respect and a strong sense of personal power

Excessive Energy: Workaholic, perfectionist, inability to relax

Deficient Energy: Depressed and insecure

Sun Altar

I always say that an altar is very personal; it has to be for you to be able to connect with the energy. Mine (much to my husband's dismay, I have several around the house) all start out clean and neat, but I find I add things to them as time passes. You will know what needs to be put on your altar. If you aren't sure then start with a guide or suggestions from others (books, friends, I.nternet etc) but keep it simple and then live with it for a bit. You will find that you are drawn to add other items to it.

Here are some of my suggestions for a sun altar, you don't have to use all or even any of these, in fact if you put everything listed on there it would be pretty crowded, sometimes less is more.

Altar cloth; which could be a head scarf, a table cloth, napkin or bandana, it doesn't have to be an expensive item. I like to use yellow and orange colours.

Sun symbols – well that's a given really, you can get all sorts of items, ornaments and bric-a-brac in sun shapes.

Flowers – fresh, dried or imitation, go for sunny yellows, oranges and reds but any bright flowers will sit nicely.

Fruit – oranges and lemons look fabulous on an altar, you could even dry some slices to decorate with.

Crystals – go with whatever you are drawn to but if you need some guidance there is a list of sun crystals in this book.

Candles – there probably aren't many altars that don't have candles on! Go with sunny or fiery colours.

Any spells you are working on can be popped on your sun altar to give them a boost of solar energy.

Flame symbols to represent fire.

Triskelion or phoenix images.

Coloured ribbons.

Circles and discs in yellow, brass, copper or gold colours.

Equal armed crosses or the swastika.

God's eyes (see craft section on how to make one).

Oak leaves and any fresh greenery.

The Sun or Chariot tarot card.

Antlers and horns work well to bring in the masculine energy of the sun.

A wand, again for the masculine energy.

Flower wreaths, I often use my flower circlets on an altar.

Bees – not real ones obviously, how would you stop them from buzzing about?

Honey – a little dish or pot full.

If you are working with a solstice or equinox you can add in symbols and correspondences that tie in with the energy of the season.

Sun Symbols

There are various symbols and images which have been and are associated with the sun or solar energy. They can be placed on your altar in honour of solar energy or the sun gods, drawn on petition papers or inscribed into candles for candle magic. Here are some of the more recognised ones.

Triskelion

This three-legged sign is thought to represent the sun in its stages of sunrise, midday and sunset. It also represents the triple goddess, the three worlds (living, dead and spirit) and the stages of life.

Swastika

Oh, this is such a misused and misunderstood symbol when really its original meaning is full of beauty. It actually faces the opposite way to the Nazi use of the symbol; you often see it in Hindu and Buddhist temples. It is a symbol of the sun and stands for prosperity, eternity, abundance and good fortune.

Sun cross

Basically, a circle with an equilateral cross inside it. This symbol was found throughout ancient cultures and is believed to have been a solar symbol. The term 'sun cross' seems to be more modern but the image of a cross in a circle has very ancient roots, thought to symbolise the wheel of the sun god's chariot. The cross represents the four compass directions; north, east, south and west. But if you lay a cross over it diagonally you get the solstices and equinoxes too.

Ankh

I have put the familiar Egyptian symbol of the Ankh here because it represents life, as the sun does. It brings insight, fertility and wisdom along with eternal life.

Eye

The eye of Horus/Ra is very recognisable from the Egyptian stories and images, it symbolises protection and life. Horus/Ra being sun gods results in it having particular meaning when working with solar energy. A lot of cultures treat the right eye as the solar symbol and the left eye as lunar.

Spiral

This is such a simple image but one of my favourites. It symbolises life, rebirth, growth, connection to the divine, consciousness, creation and spirituality. It can lead from the material world round into the inner spirit.

Circle

Basic but brilliant. The circle is round like the sun and never-ending like the sun (well obviously it does have a shelf life but hopefully it will last us a few more millennia!). Circles represent the planet and if you get the colour right (yellow or gold) it makes an excellent representation of the sun. It is a symbol of wholeness, everything, perfection, infinity, cycles, revolution, centring and completion.

Wheel

Not only does the wheel have a connection to all the sun gods and their chariots (chariots needing wheels of course), but it is also a circle. It goes around ...and round ... as does the sun and the cycle of life.

Infinity

The infinity symbol which looks like a figure 8 laid on its side is never-ending, hence its name infinity. There is an astronomical situation where the position of the sun is traced in the sky throughout an entire year, seen from a fixed point. When you map the journey of the sun you get the infinity symbol.

The Sun Tarot Card

One of the major arcana, the Sun tarot card is always a joy to receive in a reading. But it can be used as a signifier or focus point for spell work or meditation if you want to connect with the energy of the sun.

Keywords for the Sun tarot card are: Success, positive energy, vitality, fun, optimism, fulfilment, happiness, enthusiasm, strength, goals, achievements, inner child.

The card is often depicted with children playing happily as it does signify letting your inner child out and the happiness and joy that comes with allowing yourself to just enjoy life. It is a card that shouts success, abundance and happy endings. But also, one of action, enthusiasm, strength and energy. It is a beautiful card that shows confidence and get up and go. The sun is shining upon you and life is good. No need for anything complicated or to over think things, you can see the sun lighting up the way for you, it brings clarity and allows you to move forward in a very positive way.

Use the Sun tarot card as your focus for meditation if you need clarity on a situation or want to see which clear pathway to take. Let the card take you on a journey to find some direction.

Solar Offerings

If you want the sun to lend its energy to you or to your spell work or if you want to call upon a solar deity to give you a hand, I think it is always polite to give an offering. It might be that you put out an offering before you ask or give one as thanks afterwards, or better still both.

Ground and centre and still your mind and ask what offerings are required. You may find that words, ideas or images pop into your head. Sometimes it might seem a bit weird (my goddess, the Cailleach, once insisted I find a potted plant to put on her altar and she was very specific about what she wanted) but go with the flow.

If you are stuck, here are some suggestions, leave them outside if you don't have any worry about animals or children disturbing or eating them. If you are popping your offerings outside in your garden or in a natural area PLEASE make sure they are biodegradable, plastic, fabric, ribbons tied to trees and candles should not be left outside in nature. Or pop them on your altar indoors. If you can leave them outside then all the better, you are working with the sun after all!

Crystals – from the list in this book or one you are drawn to.

Herbs – dried or fresh.

Plants and flowers – dried or fresh.

Food – honey, wine, orange juice, beer or mead works well for solar offerings, left out in a little dish or pour some onto the ground.

Cake or bread – again left out in a dish or crumbled over the ground.

Barley or wheat.

Chocolate (note: chocolate melts in the sun, it can be very deceptive … it looks like a whole firm block of chocolate, then you go to pick it up and actually it is molten lava).

If I am making an offering for a specific intent or to a particular deity I often make up a blend, as I would do when making a loose incense. I mix together dried flowers, herbs and spices and add in maybe a few seeds or a crystal and pop it on my outside altar or in the garden.

Rainbows

(from my book *Witchcraft into the Wilds*)

Such a beautiful and magical sight and although we can't actually pick, cut, dry or bottle rainbows they can still be used in magic. There are even one or two rainbow deities such as the Greek goddess Iris, the Rainbow Serpent who is the creator in the Dreaming from Aboriginal beliefs and in Norse mythology Midgard (Earth) and Asgard (home of the gods) is connected by means of the Bifrost which is a burning rainbow bridge. In some Native American traditions, the rainbow is believed to be a pathway of the holy spirits and in Japanese cultures the rainbow was believed to be the bridge that their ancestors took to descend to earth.

What makes a rainbow? It is all about reflection, refraction and dispersion of light in water droplets. When sunlight beams down it appears to be white even though it is actually made up of different colours that we don't usually see but when that beam of light hits raindrops on the way down at a specific angle, the different colours that make up the beam separate to form a rainbow. Rainbows caused by sunlight always appear in the section of the sky directly opposite the sun.

There are supposedly seven colours of the rainbow: red, orange, yellow, green, blue, indigo and violet. Apparently these colours were suggested by Sir Isaac Newton so who are we to argue? Seven, of course, being a magical number as well.

The colours can obviously be used with colour magic, but did you know you can also sing the rainbow? Singing the sound of each colour can also be worked into your spells:

Red – do
Orange – re
Yellow – mi

Green – fa
Blue – sol
Indigo – la
Violet – si/ti

And of course, if you work with chakras the colours of the rainbow are represented by the seven main chakras – with indigo being purple and violet being white.

Red – root/base
Orange – sacral
Yellow – solar plexus
Green – heart
Blue – throat
Indigo/purple – third eye
Violet/white – crown

So, rainbows bring the magic of water, sunlight and colour. The rainbow usually appears after the rain, so it brings hope, promise and healing. As it is a combination of water and sun energy, I think it also works on an emotional level too. The rainbow also appears to be a connection between the earth and the skies or the divine, so it works well for spirit or deity magic as well.

The rainbow has also been used as a symbol of diversity and I think that makes perfect sense, it brings together all of the colours to make something beautiful, so it can also work magic for strength, resilience, co-operation, acceptance and harmony.

I also think that the rainbow is something that not only includes the colours we use in artistic endeavours but as it is often painted by children it brings the magic of creativity, inspiration and lets out our inner child.

Apparently, it is known to be bad luck to point at a rainbow...

You can place magical items or tools at the end of the rainbow to charge and cleanse them – obviously it is difficult to actually find the real end of a rainbow (along with the pot of gold) but you could place your item on a windowsill or wall where it looks like the rainbow is heading into it.

Take a photograph of the rainbow and use it in blessing magical workings.

Rainbow Meditation

Make yourself comfortable in a place where you won't be disturbed.

Close your eyes and focus on your breathing, deep breaths in ... deep breaths out.

As your world around you dissipates you find yourself sitting on flat grey rocks.

You are surrounded by stone cliffs on two sides; a lush green valley is spread out behind you and in front of you is the most amazing g waterfall.

The sky above you is a clear blue and the sun is shining.

Take a proper look at your surrounds, feel the stone beneath you and take in the green grass and wild flowers that fill the valley.

Take a deep breath in and fill your lungs with the fresh sweet scent of the air.

You can hear birds and cattle away behind you in the distance of the valley.

And the sound of the waterfall as it cascades down into a pool is wonderful.

You gaze into the pool in front of you and see the stones and pebbles on the bed beneath the clear water. There are also gorgeous multi coloured fish swimming around just under the surface.

As you look up you follow the water as if falls from the top of the cliff. Your eye catches something and you realise there is a beautiful, breath taking rainbow curving across from the top of the waterfall down into the pool beneath.

The colours shimmer in the sunlight and reflect on the water.

Take in all the different shades of colour.

Focus on the point where the rainbow hits the pool of water and make a wish ...

Wait for a moment ... you may see a sign or hear some words.

Bask in the sun, listen to the water and take your time soaking up your surroundings.

When you are ready open your eyes and slowly come back to this reality.

Wriggle your fingers and toes, drink some water and grab something to eat.

Solar Spells

You can use the sun energy in all sorts of spells, create and work your magic outside in the sunshine, charge your tools and crystals in the rays of the sun and call upon the sun or solar deities to lend their energy to your workings.

Here are some spells that call upon sun magic.

Sun shield spell
Stand outside in the sunshine. Visualise a bubble of gold energy surrounding you. Visualise the rays of the sun coming down and filling the bubble, strengthening the outer area of the bubble. You can use this personal protection shield whenever you feel the need.

Energy spell
Stand outside in the sunshine. Keep your eyes closed but turn your face to the sun. Allow the energy from the sun to fill your body. Let it course through your veins, cleansing and energising. When you feel ready clap your hands and stamp your feet to allow any excess energy to drain into the soil.

Goal tarot spell
Using the Sun tarot card and picking a crystal of your choice, write your goal, be specific on a slip of paper, something you would like to achieve or have more of in your life. Lay it on your altar (or somewhere that it won't be disturbed). Take the Sun tarot card and say out loud your request, holding the card in front of you. Place the tarot card on top of your slip of paper. Charge the crystal in your hand with the same desire and pop that on top of the tarot card. Leave it in place for seven days, re-charging the crystal and re-energising the spell by saying your desire out loud at least once a day. On the seventh day burn or

bury the slip of paper and cleanse the card and crystal for re-use. To add extra solar power, you could start this spell on a Sunday. Let the sun do its thing ...

Solar crystal spell

Pick a crystal that represents solar magic to you, go outside at sunrise (or early morning if sunrise isn't possible) and hold the crystal in your hand, lift it up to the sun. Say a chant or some words asking for the energy from the sun. See the energy being directed down from the sun into your crystal. Leave the crystal out in the sun or on the window sill. Go back outside at midday and repeat. Do the same thing again at sunset. Carry the crystal with you for positive sunny energy. Recharge when you feel it is necessary.

Solar candle spell

This is a multi-purpose spell that can be used for any intent that corresponds to solar energy.

You will need:

A candle (colour of your choice)

A crystal of your choice

Herbs to correspond with your intent

Set your candle outside in the sunshine in a safe place on a fireproof dish. Charge the crystal with your intent and pop it in front of the candle. Charge the herbs with your intent and sprinkle them around the candle. Light the candle and sit quietly visualising your desires and goals. Ask the sun to lend its energy to the spell. Sit with the candle until it burns out. Sprinkle the herbs on the ground and take the crystal with you.

To add power to your spell, time it with the sun's position in the sky: sunrise for new projects and beginnings, midday for power and strength and sunset to release and let go.

A sunset releasing spell

Either sit outside so that you can see the sunset or get in a position where you can see it through your window.

You will need:

Four candles – colours of your choice but I suggest tying them in with the colours of a sunset (yellow, orange, pink and red). If you don't have coloured candles, white will be fine.

Four slips of paper and a pen

Fireproof dish

Light all four candles.

Write down on each slip of paper what it is you would like to let go of. It only needs to be a word or two.

Set fire to a slip of paper from the first candle and pop it in the fireproof dish to burn. Take another slip of paper and set fire to it from the second candle and pop it in the dish to burn. Repeat with the third and fourth candle.

You might like to say a chant each time, or just request out loud what your intent is.

Then snuff out the candles in reverse order.

Finally look towards the sun as it sets below the horizon and say out loud 'the end of my woes, ready for the beginning of a new day'.

A sunrise fresh start spell

Using the sunset spell as a template, you can work the spell as the sun begins to rise at the beginning of the day, using the intent for new beginnings or a fresh start.

You will need:

Four candles – colours of your choice but I suggest tying them in with the colours of a sunrise (pale yellow, white, baby pink and pale blue). If you don't have coloured candles, white will be fine.

Four slips of paper and a pen

Fireproof dish

Light all four candles.

Write down on each slip of paper what it is you would like to start, a new project, a fresh beginning or something you would like to increase. It only needs to be a word or two.

Set fire to a slip of paper from the first candle and pop it in the fireproof dish to burn. Take another slip of paper and set fire to it from the second candle and pop it in the dish to burn. Repeat with the third and fourth candle.

You might like to say a chant each time, or just request out loud what your intent is.

Then snuff out the candles in reverse order.

Finally look towards the sun as it rises and say out loud 'as the sun begins to rise, new beginnings and fresh starts I surmise'. Or something much better than my meagre poetry skills can manage!

Phoenix Spell to rise from the flames

What you need:

A statue or picture of a phoenix

A red or orange candle

Pop the image of the phoenix behind the candle and light the flame. Focus on the phoenix; take in every detail, the colours and shapes. Get the image really clear in your mind. State your challenges or issues to the phoenix; ask it to help you let go of the troubles and blockages and move forward triumphant.

Listen for any messages and watch for any images as you focus on the image and the flame from the candle.

When you are ready finish up with a chant, something like:

Phoenix full of life and fire

Help and aid me and my desire
Burn away all that holds me back
Give me the courage and confidence that I lack.

Snuff out the flame and keep the image of the phoenix with you (if it is a photo) or on your altar, somewhere that you will see it regularly and be reminded of how strong you are.

Celebrating the Sun

Obviously the most straightforward idea is to go outside and soak up the sun's rays (not for too long if it is very hot and don't forget your sunscreen). But here are some other suggestions:

Drawing down the sun (see section in this book).

Place a yellow candle on your altar to represent the sun.

Start each day by facing the direction of the rising sun and offering up your thanks.

Charge distilled water in the sunlight and use it for magical workings.

Create solar crafts and symbols (such as a god's eye, see craft section).

Hang sun catchers in your windows.

Ancient stone circles have often been found to line up with the summer and winter solstices, create your own miniature sun stone circle in your garden using pebbles.

Charge your magical tools in the midday sun.

Grow flowers and plants in your garden that are ruled by the sun.

Add sun herbs and foods to your meals.

Create a sun magic ritual to be held outside.

Put a bright yellow cloth on your altar.

Place yellow flowers in a vase.

Create a sun crystal grid.

Make your own set of solar runes (instructions in this book).

Research and meditate with solar deities.

Work with your solar plexus chakra.

Have a picnic outside.

Sun Meditation

Make yourself comfortable in a place where you won't be disturbed.

Close your eyes and focus on your breathing, deep breaths in and long breaths out ...

As your world around you dissipates you find yourself on top of a mountain, the ground beneath your feet is covered in lush green grass and scattered with pretty wild flowers. The air is warm, and you feel comfortable.

At the moment the sky is fairly dark, and you realise it is just before day break. You turn slowly around in a circle surveying the land that lies out like a patchwork carpet before you on all sides. You can just make out the beautiful fields full of crops, grassland filled with wild flowers and a river winding its way dividing up the land.

You take a deep breath in and feel your lungs filling up with fresh sweet-scented air.

You notice behind you a blanket laid out on the grass with a large picnic hamper beside it. You sit down and open the lid to find it full of delicious looking food and drink. Ready for you to eat and drink whenever you wish.

As you watch, the sun begins to creep up above the horizon, casting a beautiful soft light across the landscape, allowing you to see the scenery in full detail.

You sit quietly watching as the sun gradually lights up the entire scene.

As the sun rises your head fills with thoughts, ideas and new inspirations. You think about each one with a clear and open mind.

As the morning wears on, the sun has now risen to great heights and is shining down from directly above you. It is midday and your mind is filled with more thoughts and ideas, how you can progress from beginnings to put projects into action.

You spend some time looking at the beauty that surrounds

you from your mountain top vantage, processing the insights you have been given.

As the sun begins to set behind you, your mind turns to those things that don't serve you, the issues, patterns and behaviours that you would like to let go of. Allow the setting sun to take them with it as it begins to dip down again below the horizon.

Eventually you are in the dark light that is dusk. You take one last look around at your view and give thanks to the energy and power of the sun.

When you are ready, slowly come back to this reality. Wriggle your fingers and toes and have a glass of water and something to eat.

Jot down all of the thoughts and insights that you had during the meditation ... and follow them up!

Solar Divination

Heliomancy, Heliomantia, Solmancy or Solmantia are all names for divination using the sun or interpreting the patterns formed by the sun's rays. You watch the rays of sunlight and the shadows produced and make your predictions based on what you see. Another method is to stand outside and close your eyes, now turn your face to the sun (keep your eyes firmly closed). Ask your question. You should get colours behind your eye lids. Note which colours you see and then decide what the colours mean to you. Red might be yes, blue may mean no. Don't face the sun for too long though!

Sun Runes

You can create your own set of sun runes (or cards if you are feeling particularly crafty).

You will need:

Pebbles, shells, crystal tumble stones, small slices of wood or glass pebbles.

Acrylic paint or permanent markers.

Think about the phases of the sun and any symbols that you associate with solar energy and assign each one a keyword and a meaning. You could also make a set using images of crystals or animals that all correspond to the sun.

Then you can charge your divination set in the sunlight.

Use them as you would runes, casting them on a flat surface for a reading or drawing one from a bag to get the answer to a question.

Here are my suggestions but get creative and personalise them for your own set.

Sunrise – New beginnings, cleansing, find a direction

Midday – Health, energy, wisdom

Sunset – Release and let go, purification

Eclipse – Positive change, transformations

Rainbow – Pathways, hope, promise

Sun cross – Directions, choices, decisions

Clouds – Hidden, secrets, judgement

Eye – Knowledge, seek the truth, clarity

Wheel – Movement, speed, travel

Infinity – Longevity, time, love

Spiral – Journey, spirituality, divine

Triskelion – Life, living, do it!

Circle – Completion, comfort, happiness

The images don't need to be complicated or detailed, you could even just write the words.

Sun Superstitions & Myths

The belief in the Aegean Islands is that when the sun sets each night it returns to the Underworld kingdom where he lives in a huge castle, received by his mother who waits for him with forty loaves of bread. If his mother is not there, then the sun eats his whole family instead. If the sun is red when it rises the next morning, then they believe he has eaten his mother. Charming ...

A red sunset has inspired many different myths such as the red is caused by the blood flowing from the Sun God as he heads to his own suicide.

The ancient Greeks thought the sun was a symbol of great beauty and would paint sun images on the cheeks of new brides.

Several cultures believed that the sun was an all-seeing eye and that no deed, good or bad could escape detection from the sun's view.

The Finns believed that the rays of the sun lead up to the place of the dead. They would send messages to the sun to pass on to those that had died.

Ancient Greeks believed that as the sun set the red hue in the sky was caused by the solar planet looking upon the blazing fires of hell and the red was the reflection from the flames.

To our ancestors the sun was incredibly important, so they would have watched it for signs and omens. If the sun had a red tinge then it was thought to be a sign of impending doom, possibly even the end of the world. A beige/light brown hue would suggest that food would be scarce, and a famine was on the horizon. And of course, a solar eclipse when the sun went dark was the final judgement and the end of days.

Pagans often use the term deosil which means to walk or move in a sunwise or clockwise motion. There is a tradition in Scotland of 'making the deazil' which involves walking three times around a person in a sunwise direction, this will bring them good luck and fortune. To walk in the opposite or anti-clockwise (widdershins) direction will bring bad luck and misfortune.

The Tungusic people have a tradition of making an accused man walk toward the sun holding a knife and shouting 'If I am guilty, may the sun send sickness to rage in my bowels like this knife' … sounds messy.

In Mexico it is believed that the head of the bed must never be in the direction of the sunrise as it will cause bad headaches and possibly even insanity.

In Germany on St John's Day, hunters that wish to have a good season fire at the sun. It is also believed that doing this will condemn the shooter to hunt forever and ever and ever … make your choice.

A Greek tale tells of the Fates and how they predicted that on coming into her fifteenth year of age a princess must be careful never to let the sun shine upon her, otherwise she may turn into a lizard.

If the sun shines on a bride on her wedding day it is thought to be good luck.

If the sun shines whilst it is also raining then witches are baking cakes … I bake cakes on any day, never mind the weather.

Streaks of sunlight coming through clouds means that rain is on the way. The sun is said to be 'pulling up moisture'.

And to the Dark Side ...

As with most things, there is positive and a negative, a black and a white, a good and a bad side. All things in balance. I have discussed all the positive sides of working sun magic and there are many – it is a hugely powerful resource just waiting for us to tap into it to gain insight, guidance and support. But it also has a dark side. The sun is, after all, a big ball of fire and with that comes the power for destruction.

I expect that we have all felt the power of the sun on occasion when we have been out in it too long or forgotten to put on sun lotion. It burns your skin and it can be incredibly painful for humans and animals alike. In extreme cases it can be incredibly dangerous.

The sun has also been known to aid forest fires. Too much long hot weather and no rain can dry out woodland and grassland areas to the point where just a spark or even the sun shining through glass can create a fire. If it gets out of hand it can become a catastrophe of epic proportions.

Basic common-sense rules apply. Don't stay out in the sun unprotected for too long. Be careful leaving glass items out in the sunshine (and that includes hanging glass objects in windows). And as a side note – don't leave candles on windowsills ... the sun melts them.

Fire of course is incredibly destructive but if used wisely can be cleansing and purifying. Burning down and removing all of the old to make way for the new, just be very careful when setting fires. Make sure you have the skill and materials to keep them contained. NEVER leave a fire or candle unattended.

Solar Crafts

A god's eye

This was one of the very first pagan crafts I made, and it is really simple but incredibly effective. In my research it does seem to have a bit of an eclectic background, a bit of a mish mash by all accounts. It does seem to have always been a spiritual object. They can be found in Mexico as Ojo de Dios, the 'all seeing' and that which understands everything, but also brings protection. One tradition I found is the creation of a God's eye when a child is born, then a layer is added for every year of the child's life until they reach the age of five. They do seem to have been adopted by the pagan community to represent the gods, masculine and solar energy. The four points of the God's Eye could also be used to represent the four elements. It looks like an equal wooden cross with a square pattern of yarn.

You will need:

Two sticks (pieces of wood, skewers, coffee stirrers, twigs or chopsticks)

Wool, string or yarn (I have also made them with thin coloured ribbon)

Mix it up colour-wise but if you are making a God's eye specifically to represent solar energy, I suggest going with the obvious yellows, reds and oranges – but go with what you are drawn to use or what you have!

Start by crossing two sticks to form an equal cross shape.

Secure the sticks and keep them in place by wrapping a piece of yarn around the intersecting points of the stick. Tie a knot to start or just tuck the tail under the yarn as you start to wrap. Do a few wraps in one direction and then rotate your sticks and do a few wraps in the other direction to fix them in place.

Then start creating ... wrap the yarn around one stick, close to the centre and take it over to the next stick, wrap it around that stick and then take it to the next stick. Continue wrapping and winding, rotating the craft as you work. You can wrap the yarn over the sticks or under, it doesn't matter as long as you are consistent.

If you want to change to a new colour yarn, cut the yarn you were using and tie it to the new piece of yarn. Trim the ends and continue wrapping. Make sure you tuck the knot to the back of the craft.

When you are finished wrap the yarn around the last stick and tie, cut leaving a piece of yarn long enough to make a loop to hang it from.

If you are feeling really crafty you can also work beads into the design as you go.

If you want to work magic into your craft, visualise and/or chant your intent as you wrap the yarn.

Sun mobiles

There are all sorts of fabulous things you can hang onto string, wire or ribbon to create a sun mobile to hang in your garden or your window.

Crystals, beads, tiny craft mirrors, buttons or discs filled with tissue paper – be creative!

Hang strings of beads from twigs.

Use fishing line and string beads, mirrors and shells to hang in your window.

Make sun shapes using paper plates and tissue paper.

Shape wire into sun symbols.

If you can crochet or knit – create sun shapes and string them together to make a mobile or bunting.

Sun tiles

Create tiles with painted images and symbols of the sun, to use on your altar, as candle holders or in the garden. You can often buy odd tiles from hardware/home depots for a few pence. Or make your own tiles from salt dough and paint them. Paint on simple sun shapes, flowers or sun symbols. If you want them to last, coat them in varnish.

Melted crayon hanging

Hang this in your window to allow the sun to shine through it.

You will need:
A sheet of white paper
4 to 5 small crayon bits in various colours
Crayon sharpener or cheese grater
Pencil
Scissors
Metal pie/cake tin
Tape
Hole punch
String

Grate or sharpen the crayon so that you have a pile of shavings. You will need a total of approximately 5 teaspoons. Place the pie tin onto the paper and draw around it. Cut the circle out and pop it into the bottom of the tin. Secure with a couple of pieces of tape.

Sprinkle the crayon shavings over the paper and place the tin outside under direct sunlight.

Keep an eye on it, if it is a very warm day it won't take long for the sun to melt the shavings so that they all meld together.

Allow it to cool slightly and then remove the circle of paper from the pie tin. Punch a hole at the top and thread with string to hang it in your window.

Sunshine prints

The sun will change the colour of your images … as if by magic!

You will need:
1 sheet black construction paper
Several small objects (anything you want)
Baking sheet
Tape
Spray bottle
1 tablespoon lemon juice
1/2 cup water

Find some small objects; they might be scissors, buttons, coins, toy animals, interestingly shaped ornaments etc. They need to have a little bit of weight to them so that they won't blow away. Place the black paper onto the baking sheet and secure with a couple of pieces of tape. Arrange the items onto the paper in an interesting pattern. Mix the water and lemon juice in the spray bottle and then lightly spray over the objects. Place the sheet outside in the sun. The lemon juice and water act as a bleaching agent when heated by the sun. A few hours later you can remove the objects and you should be left with their images on the paper.

Sun Magic Recipes

Sunflower biscuits
450g (1 lb) plain (all-purpose) flour
2 pinches salt
225g (8oz) butter (or lard)
4–6 tablespoons cold water
175g (6oz) smooth peanut butter (or chocolate spread)
175g (6oz) granulated sugar
Red food colouring

Preheat the oven to 180C/350F/Gas 4 and butter a baking sheet or put a sheet of baking parchment on top.

Pop the flour into a bowl, add the salt and butter and rub together until they resemble breadcrumbs. Then add the cold water a little at a time and combine until the pastry forms a ball. Roll the dough into a sausage shape and cut into 12 equal slices and roll into balls.

To make the filling mix the peanut butter with the sugar. Flatten the balls of pastry into discs and fill each one with a spoonful of the filling. Seal up the edges turn over and pat flat.

Paint a red dot on the middle of each disc and let the food colouring dry. Then put twelve incisions in the pastries around the edge of the red dot and twist each 'petal' to the right.

Pop them onto the baking tray and bake for 15–20 minutes until golden brown.

Solar shortbread cookies
This is the base recipe then you can add in different flavours, herbs or spices. This recipe can be used to make the four different cookies used in the sun ritual in this book.

Ingredients:

    1 cup (8oz/240g) butter, room temperature

    1/2 cup (2oz/60g)) icing sugar/powdered sugar

    2 cups (10oz/300g) plain/all-purpose flour

Preheat your oven to 350F/180C/Gas 4 and line a baking tray with parchment paper.

In a large bowl cream together the soft butter and sugar until light and fluffy.

Add in the flour and mix until the dough just comes together. If you are adding in flavours, pop them in at this stage.

Turn the dough out onto a board/surface dusted with icing/powdered sugar and gently roll the dough into a long two by two-inch log.

Wrap the log of cookie dough in cling/plastic wrap and allow to firm up in the fridge for 30 minutes.

Once the dough is firm, slice the cookies into ¾ inch thick rounds. Place each round on your baking tray and bake for 16–18 minutes or until just golden.

Allow to cool slightly before transferring to a cooling rack.

Once cool the cookies can be stored in an air tight container for up to 3 days.

Ginger cookies – add one teaspoon ground ginger

    Honey cookies – add one teaspoon honey

    Cinnamon cookies – add one teaspoon ground cinnamon

    Orange or lemon cookies – add the zested rind of one orange or one lemon

Vegan shortbread cookies

This is a vegan version that can have different flavours added.

Ingredients:

    40g (1/3 cup) icing/powdered sugar

100g (1/2 cup) coconut oil, hard

1/4 to 1/2 teaspoon salt

165g (1 1/3 cup) plain/all-purpose flour

3 tablespoons non-dairy milk – although you may not need this, only add if you really cannot get it to come together without as it affects the texture of the shortbread.

Preheat oven to 350°F/180C/Gas 4 and line a baking sheet with parchment paper.

Combine the icing/powdered sugar, salt and the coconut oil in a bowl. Use a fork to mash together really well or whizz in the food mixer until it is light and fluffy.

Mix in the flour until everything is combined. Don't over mix as it will affect the texture of the finished cookie. Add any flavouring at this point, if using.

Add the milk only if you need to bring the dough together. It should be slightly crumbly but hold together if you squeeze it together in your hand. The drier you can get away with keeping the dough, the better the texture of your shortbread, if you do, add it very gradually.

Lightly dust a surface with flour and shape your dough into a ball. Roll out to about 3–4 mm thick then use a cookie cutter to cut into shapes.

Place gently on the prepared cookie sheet.

Bake for 10–12 minutes. They will start turning a little golden around the edges when done.

Keep an eye on them in the last few minutes as they can turn from okay to overdone very quickly. They will still feel slightly soft in the middle when done but will firm up as they cool.

Place them on a cooling rack to cool.

Lemon and poppy seed cake

Two fabulous flavours come together for this lush cake.

For the sponge:
225g (8oz) unsalted butter, softened, plus more for the tins
225g (8oz) caster sugar
4 large eggs
225g (8oz) plain (all-purpose) flour
2 teaspoons baking powder
3 unwaxed lemons, zest finely grated, reserving a few slivers
    for decoration
1 unwaxed lemon, juiced
50g (1 1/2 oz) poppy seeds

For the icing:
50g (1 1/2 oz) unsalted butter, softened
100g (3 1/2 oz) cream cheese or I used mascarpone
400g (14 oz) icing sugar
2 tablespoons lemon juice
4 tablespoons lemon curd

Preheat the oven to 180°C. Butter 2 x 20 cm round sandwich tins and line the bases with baking parchment. In a large bowl, beat together the sugar and butter with an electric whisk until light-coloured and creamy. Beat in the eggs one by one, beating thoroughly between each addition. If the mixture starts to split, just add 1 tablespoon of the flour and continue beating; this will bring the mixture back. Sift together the flour and baking powder and fold into the mixture with the finely grated lemon zest and poppy seeds, making sure to mix in any flour at the bottom of the bowl. Be gentle when you're folding; you don't want to knock out the air you've incorporated through all that whisking. Fold in the lemon juice and divide the batter evenly between the prepared tins, smoothing the surfaces. Bake for 18–20 minutes, or until a cocktail stick comes out clean when poked into the centre of each cake. When the tins have cooled enough to handle, turn out the sponges and cool on a wire rack.

Meanwhile, prepare the icing. Beat together the butter and cream cheese in a large bowl with the electric whisk until creamy and fully combined. Beat in half the icing sugar (start your whisk on slow, or you'll get icing sugar all over the kitchen). Beat in the lemon juice then gradually beat in the rest of the icing sugar, a couple of spoonfuls at a time, until it's a thick-but-spreadable consistency.

Spread the lemon curd on the bottom sponge then spread about half the icing on the bottom layer of the sponge. Try to spread it evenly and right up to the edges, so you can see a neat line of icing once the top goes on. Turn the top layer of sponge upside down and lay on top of the icing, pressing down gently and scraping off any excess icing that squidges out. Neatly spread or pipe the remaining icing on top and decorate with the remaining slivers of zest or a sprinkle of poppy seeds.

Basic vegan chocolate muffin recipe
Add different toppings or fillings such as grated citrus zest or vegan chocolate chips to this basic recipe, but it is delicious just as it is.

1 cup/8 fl oz soya or almond milk (if you use dark chocolate almond milk it tastes especially yummy)
1 teaspoon apple cider vinegar
3/4 cup/6 oz sugar
1/3 cup/2 1/2 fl oz vegetable oil
1 1/2 teaspoons vanilla extract
1 cup/ 8 oz plain (all-purpose) flour
1/3 cup/2 1/2 oz cocoa powder
3/4 teaspoon baking soda
1/2 teaspoon baking powder
1/2 teaspoon salt

Preheat the oven to 350F/180C/Gas 4.

Line a 12-hole muffin tin with paper liners.

Whisk together the milk and vinegar and leave to sit for a few minutes so that it slightly curdles. Add in the sugar, oil and vanilla to the milk and beat together until if foams. In a separate bowl mix together the flour, cocoa, baking soda, baking powder and salt. Gradually beat the flour mixture into the wet ingredients until it is well mixed. Spoon into the cake cases. Bake for 15 to 20 minutes.

Greek halva pudding

This semolina dish doesn't look the prettiest, but it tastes lush. And it is also vegan and wheat free. If you don't have measuring cups, use a mug.

1/2 cup olive oil
1/2 cup vegetable/corn oil
2 cups semolina
1/4 cup sultanas

For the syrup:
3 cups of sugar
4 cups water
1 teaspoon ground cinnamon

Start by preparing the syrup. Add the syrup ingredients into a pan over a high heat and bring to the boil. Boil until the sugar has dissolved and the syrup slightly thickens. Set aside but keep warm.

To prepare the halva, heat the oil in a large pan and gradually mix in the semolina. Stir constantly to allow the semolina to absorb the oil. When the semolina starts to bubble turn the heat down and allow it to toast until golden (keep stirring). Be careful not to over toast it otherwise it will taste bitter. Remove the pan from the heat and pour in the warm syrup. Stir and return the pan to the heat. Cook whilst stirring until the mixture thickens and pulls away easily from the sides of the pan.

Remove the pan from the heat and stir in the sultanas. Cover the halva with a tea towel and let it rest for ten minutes. Then pour the mixture into a serving dish. Allow to cool for a couple of hours.

And Finally, to the Sunset ...

Whatever way you choose to work with the sun and its solar energy, have fun with it. Make it personal to you and work in a way that fills your heart and soul with happiness.

MOON

BOOKS

PAGANISM & SHAMANISM

What is Paganism? A religion, a spirituality, an alternative
belief system, nature worship? You can find support for all these
definitions (and many more) in dictionaries, encyclopaedias, and
text books of religion, but subscribe to any one and the truth will
evade you. Above all Paganism is a creative pursuit, an encounter
with reality, an exploration of meaning and an expression of the
soul. Druids, Heathens, Wiccans and others, all contribute their
insights and literary riches to the Pagan tradition. Moon Books
invites you to begin or to deepen your own encounter, right here,
right now.

If you have enjoyed this book, why not tell other readers by
posting a review on your preferred book site.

Medicine for the Soul
The Complete Book of Shamanic Healing
Ross Heaven
All you will ever need to know about shamanic healing and how to
become your own shaman...
Paperback: 978-1-78099-419-2 ebook: 978-1-78099-420-8

Shaman Pathways – The Druid Shaman
Exploring the Celtic Otherworld
Danu Forest
A practical guide to Celtic shamanism with exercises and
techniques as well as traditional lore for exploring the Celtic
Otherworld.
Paperback: 978-1-78099-615-8 ebook: 978-1-78099-616-5

Traditional Witchcraft for the Woods and Forests
A Witch's Guide to the Woodland with Guided Meditations and
Pathworking
Melusine Draco
A Witch's guide to walking alone in the woods, with guided
meditations and pathworking.
Paperback: 978-1-84694-803-9 ebook: 978-1-84694-804-6

Wild Earth, Wild Soul
A Manual for an Ecstatic Culture
Bill Pfeiffer
Imagine a nature-based culture so alive and so connected,
spreading like wildfire. This book is the first flame...
Paperback: 978-1-78099-187-0 ebook: 978-1-78099-188-7

Naming the Goddess
Trevor Greenfield
Naming the Goddess is written by over eighty adherents and
scholars of Goddess and Goddess Spirituality.
Paperback: 978-1-78279-476-9 ebook: 978-1-78279-475-2

Shapeshifting into Higher Consciousness
Heal and Transform Yourself and Our World with Ancient
Shamanic and Modern Methods
Llyn Roberts
Ancient and modern methods that you can use every day to
transform yourself and make a positive difference in the world.
Paperback: 978-1-84694-843-5 ebook: 978-1-84694-844-2

Readers of ebooks can buy or view any of these bestsellers by
clicking on the live link in the title. Most titles are published in
paperback and as an ebook. Paperbacks are available in traditional
bookshops. Both print and ebook formats are available online.

Find more titles and sign up to our readers' newsletter at
http://www.johnhuntpublishing.com/paganism
Follow us on Facebook at https://www.facebook.com/MoonBooks
and Twitter at https://twitter.com/MoonBooksJHP